ONEIDA COMMUNITY PROFILES

A York State Book

ONEIDA
COMMUNITY
PROFILES

Constance Noyes Robertson

 SYRACUSE UNIVERSITY PRESS   1977

Library of Congress Cataloging in Publication Data

Robertson, Constance Noyes.
  Oneida Community profiles.

  1. Oneida Community. I. Title.
HX656.05R633   335'.9'74764   77-8226
ISBN 0-8156-0140-9

Manufactured in the United States of America

CONTENTS

Preface   vii

The Road to Oneida   1

The Cragins   27

Building the Oneida Community   47

Self-Improvement   55

The Branch Communes   65

The Wordens   79

The Second Putney Commune   95

The Crystal Palace   107

Disastrous Events   115

Wisdom and Righteousness   137

CONSTANCE NOYES ROBERTSON, granddaughter of John Humphrey Noyes, has lived most of her life in the Oneida area and has known many members of the old Community. Both her parents belonged to the Oneida Community generation called Stirpicults, and her father, Pierrepont B. Noyes, played an important part in reanimating the joint-stock company that succeeded the old Community, now the modern silversmiths, Oneida Limited. Mrs. Robertson is the author of nine published novels, including a book club selection, *Firebell in the Night.*

PREFACE

IT IS DOUBTFUL IF, even with the best will in the world, the past can be recovered, but because, as a community, Oneida was one of the most successful as well as the most durable social experiments of its period it would seem a logical subject for study. I do not intend to make a value judgment. The Oneida Community had faults, made mistakes, finally failed, but because of my personal connection with it, as a descendant, I have had access to information, both written or oral, which illuminates the human side of what might seem merely a theological aberration. It is my ambition in this book to deal not with the Community as a whole but with the communists—how they lived, what they thought and said, how they came together, what it was like to be a member of the Oneida Community in its early days.

Fortunately for me, I have been the recipient of several unexpected strokes of good fortune, some of which I have already acknowledged in my other books—windfalls of papers which I had believed destroyed years ago; a trunkful of personal letters to and from a great-grandfather; letter-press books containing copies of letters to and from John Humphrey Noyes; private diaries kept by members and lent me by their descendants. All these fit together in my mind to make a picture of the early struggles of my grandparents and great-grandparents and their associates more than a hundred years ago. I have tried to indicate these sources as I used them. Some, I hope, will ultimately be available in microfilm. Others, being privately owned, will not, so far as I know, be open to researchers.

Probably I should admit that much of this book is strictly personal. One chapter, for example, is devoted to a general contemporary view of the radical groups, then calling themselves Perfectionists but differing wildly not only in dogma but in behavior. I have described this scenario of eccentrics as a context in which one small drama, acted out by three of John Noyes's converts, should be read. Taken alone it might appear shocking or heinous, but seen against the background of its period it was scarcely notable.

Theophilus Gates and the *Battle Ax* Letter made a great stir in their period, but they remained a landmark only as long as the Oneida Community lasted and may be found in copies of *The Witness* for 1839-41, before either the Putney or Oneida Communities had been formed. It served as a kind of manifesto of Noyes's sexual philosophy, not intended for publication but plagiarized by Gates and acted upon by his followers. The Cragin story was minutely described by George Cragin twenty years after its happening and published in the Oneida Community *Circular.* My personal connection with it is simply genealogical: The Cragins were my great-grandparents; on the other side, John Humphrey Noyes was my grandfather.

The story of the first gathering at Putney and the expulsion therefrom by the little band of converts has never had a full treatment except by George W. Noyes in *The Putney Community* which contains, fortunately, letters to and from members of the Oneida group and outside friends—or occasionally enemies—the originals of which, so far as I know, have been lost or destroyed. The period of gathering into a community was an uphill climb but the expulsion from Eden was as swift as an avalanche. Trade at the Community's store had "got about as low as possible."

On the advice of their lawyer, John Noyes and the Cragins had removed themselves to New York City, since their presence in Putney merely inflamed the Putney Vigilance Committee. Noyes's brother-in-law, Larkin G. Mead, informed him that "it was intended to persecute the male members of your corporation for gross lewdness" and warned him that he would "be transferred from his pleasant parlour to a less pleasant tenement in the City Prison." Miller, who had been left to deal with the situation in Putney, never lost courage, although he admitted they were having "some hard pinches" which included an anonymous letter saying that if he did not leave town immediately, he would be tarred and feathered and ridden on a rail—not an empty threat to men and women who remembered the Mormon massacre at Nauvoo, Illinois, only three years before.

The several chapters telling of the group's arrival at Oneida and the consequent settling there—the building of a community home, the acquisition of new members, the experiments in various enterprises in their efforts to make a living, their organization of both men and women to cope with the problems both social and financial—have been drawn both from printed sources and from private diaries, journals, and letters.

The two Worden chapters, at Manlius and later at Putney's second settlement, are based on letters and diaries, mostly by, as he liked to sign himself, "M. Lafayette Worden," somehow preserved and given to me by my father, Worden's grandson. In the later chapters I have quoted from *Home Talks* by John Humphrey Noyes, *The Berean,* and *History of American Socialisms* by the same author. Quotations are also taken for the chapters dealing with the early days from *The Spiritual Magazine* (1846-50) and *The Free Church Circular* (1850-51) and *The Witness* (1837-42). After 1851 quotations are largely from the *Circular,* printed in either Brooklyn, New York, or at Oneida.

Struan House   Constance Noyes Robertson
Kenwood   ▮
Oneida, New York
Spring 1977

ONEIDA COMMUNITY PROFILES

THE ROAD TO ONEIDA

THE MOST POWERFUL and widespread religious revival since the days of Jonathan Edwards began in the year 1831 and was called the Great Awakening. The most popular revivalist was Charles G. Finney. Counties, towns, whole states took fire from his burning orations, and one section—mid New York State—was soon known as the Burnt-Over District. After Finney a host of other revivalists entered the field, and in the fall of 1831 one of the lesser lights conducted a four-day meeting in Putney, Vermont, the home of the Honorable John Noyes, his wife Polly Hayes Noyes and his eight children, of whom the eldest was John Humphrey, just a year out of Dartmouth College and aspiring to be a lawyer.

Young John—he was only twenty—had never been religious minded; in fact, when his mother begged him to attend the meeting, he only reluctantly agreed. Religion, he then thought, was a "sort of phrenzy to which all were liable and he feared lest he should be caught in the snare"—which, one might say, was exactly what happened. Seven days later he experienced conversion and, as he later wrote, "Light gleamed upon my soul in a different way from what I had expected. It was dim and almost imperceptible at first but in the course of the day it attained meridian splendor. Ere the day was done I had concluded to devote myself to the service and ministry of God." To that service he did devote the next fifty years.

What kind of man was this passionate young convert? William James, in *Varieties of Religious Experiences*, has portrayed

him in describing "a religious genius." Other writers have called
him other things, from a crank to a crazy man, and James admitted that "a religious life, exclusively pursued does tend to make
the person exceptional and eccentric . . . a pattern-maker, an original to whom religion was not a dull habit but an acute fever. If
there is such a thing as inspiration from a higher realm, it might
well be that the neurotic temperament would furnish the chief
condition of the requisite receptivity."

It was said in the family that John, like his mother, never
did things by halves. Without a backward glance, having decided to
devote his life to God, he abandoned his study of law and enrolled
in the Andover Theological Seminary. One year there convinced
him that the school lacked seriousness, and he transferred to the
Yale Theological Seminary, from which he graduated in 1833.
During the next year of almost ceaseless study and argument, both
with the faculty of the Seminary and with a group of young radicals, he developed his theory that perfection was obtainable and,
preaching at the New Haven Free Church, on February 20, 1834,
he made his announcement: "He that committeth sin is of the
devil."

It can only be imagined how, in the boiling ferment of that
period, this astounding declaration was received. As Noyes wrote
later in his *Confession of Religious Experience*, "Within a few
hours the word passed through the college and city. 'Noyes says he
is perfect' and on the heels of this went the report: 'Noyes is
crazy.'"

"During those first days I certainly did not regard myself
as perfect in any such sense as excludes the expectation of discipline and improvement. The distinction between being free from
sin on the one hand and being past improvement on the other was
plain to me. To those who endeavored to confound the distinction
and crowd me into a profession of unimprovable perfection I said:
'I do not pretend to perfection in externals. I only claim purity of
heart and the answer of a good conscience toward God.'" At a
special meeting of the Faculty of the Seminary it was resolved that
"without impeaching the Christian character of Mr. Noyes, this
Association do hereby recall his license to preach the gospel." This
did not daunt him. When asked whether he would continue to
preach, now that the clergy had taken away his license, he replied,
"I have taken away their license to sin and they keep on sinning.

So, though they have taken away my license to preach, I shall keep on preaching."

Noyes's conclusion was that entire salvation from sin in this world had been attained by the Apostolic Church in A.D. 70 and must again emerge as the standard of Christianity. The development of this doctrine from theory to physical realization took place in Putney, Vermont, at the home of Noyes's family, in 1838. There Perfectionism first assumed the form of Association in the small family circle and its immediate connections where John Humphrey, his wife, and several members of his family joined him both in religious faith and the business of editing and printing a religious paper entitled *The Witness.*

As the *First Annual Report of the Oneida Community* put it, in 1849: "From 1840 to 1847 there was a gradual accession of members until the group numbered nearly forty. During the same period all the leading principles of the present social theory were worked out, theoretically and practically, and step by step the school advanced from community of faith to community of householding and community of affections."

Almost from the time of his first discovery, inspiration, afflatus, whatever he called it, John Noyes had been convinced that the most effective method of spreading his new gospel was through the press. He had tried preaching, going, often on foot, the length and breadth of New England, wearing himself almost to death in the effort which brought in too little return. In *The Perfectionist,* once more, in Putney in 1845, he had spent his time and all the money he could raise in this effort. In 1847, in Putney again, he brought together all that he had written in these more ephemeral journals into one volume which he called *The Berean,* taking his title from the passage in *Acts 17,* which describes the people of Berea as "more noble than those in Thessalonica, in that they receive the word with all readiness of mind."

The publication of this book created opposition, denunciation, and further schisms in the disparate and amorphous groups of Perfectionists, east and west. Legality, in Noyes's view, was also of the devil, "synonymous with restraint, compulsion, prohibition, while the spirit rules by grace and truth."

To the conventionally religious, probably his most heterodox claim was that the Second Coming of Jesus Christ had taken place in the generation of the Apostles, at the time of the destruction of Jerusalem, in A.D. 70. This had both won and lost him converts in his early days, but ten years later in Putney, his newly evolved Social Theory was the prime bone of contention, and the publication of *The Berean*, restating all his former heresies, was a challenge flung in their faces.

The original statement of this social theory, so-called, was published after their move to Oneida, in their *First Annual Report*, in 1849 and was titled *The Bible Argument*. This original and closely reasoned doctrine paved the way for Noyes's second innovation, Complex Marriage. "In the Kingdom of Heaven, the institution of marriage which assigns the exclusive possession of one woman to one man does not exist [Matt. 22:23-30] for in the resurrection they neither marry nor are given in marriage but are as the Angels of God in Heaven." The intimate union of life and interest, which in the world is limited to pairs, extends through the whole body of believers; i.e., complex marriage takes the place of simple. "The new commandment is that we love one another, and that not by pairs, as in this world, but *en masse*."

After fathering five infants, four of them stillborn, in the first six years of his marriage, John Humphrey Noyes rebelled from the accepted belief that "Nature must take its course" and set himself to find a solution to this problem which had victimized women since time began. What he discovered, which he named Male Continence, was, he proclaimed, a great victory over the tyranny of Nature and one more step into the Kingdom. Today we would call it birth control or contraception. It was also one of the absolutely necessary prerequisites to the existence of a community which could not, for its first twenty years, have supported the normal statistical number of children. Male Continence made the Oneida Community possible.

It also, at the end of those twenty years, when Oneida was prospering financially, made possible another of Noyes's dearest dreams—what he named Stirpiculture. This word, coined by the Oneida Community, was a compound of *stirpes*, the Latin word for race, and *culture*, meaning cultivation with a view to improvement, or, taken together, race-culture, and the children thus produced were colloquially called stirpicults. Robert Allerton Parker, who was fortunate enough to have access to the archives of the Oneida Community before they were destroyed, has given us the best account of this experiment in *A Yankee Saint*. I quote him in part.

One hundred men and women of the Community participated in the stirpicultural experiments and eighty-one of these became parents. Fifty-eight live children were brought into the world; there were four still births. Of the fifty-one applications from men and women desiring to become parents, nine were vetoed on the ground of unfitness, and forty-two were approved. Care of the children was in accordance with the already established custom of the Community. During early infancy they remained in the care of their mothers. When able to walk, the child was admitted to the day nursery department of the Children's House, the mother continuing the night care. From the beginning of the play stage until adolescence the Children's House had complete charge, though parents visited their children and received visits from them. Much attention was given to diet, clothing, sanitation and profitable activity. In case of illness, good medical attendance and the best of nursing was immediately available. At that time, it has been estimated that (in the 'world') approximately ten out of forty-four babies died before the end of the first five-year period. Out of the fifty-eight live births during the stirpicultural period, only six deaths had occurred in September 1921, when the oldest stirpicult was fifty-two years of age and the youngest, forty-two. According to actuarial computation for 1870 the deaths of forty-five out of these fifty-eight would have been nearer normal. Selection of parents is not entirely accountable for this low death-rate. Other factors such as the exceptional care provided by the Community and excellent hygienic conditions decreased the infant mortality rate. Of the children of these stirpicults, out of a total of ninety-eight births, only three failed to survive the first twelve months, and there were no still births. Full credit must be given of course to the hardy New England stock represented in the stirpicultural matings, as well as the exceptional intelligence applied to domestic and personal hygiene in the Community house. The results are said, by actuarial experts, to be unprecedented in the records of contemporary vital statistics.

All this, of course, was twenty years in the future. Meanwhile, back in Putney in the ten years between 1838 and 1848, John Noyes was laboring to draw together the members who were to comprise what was first called the Society of Inquiry or later the Putney Corporation of Perfectionists. These, in the beginning were John Noyes's family, two sisters, a younger brother, his own new wife. Communism of property began in 1842, and in 1844 they drew up a Contract of Partnership which specified that all property of the members should be held in common as the prop-

The Squire Noyes house, boyhood home of John Humphrey Noyes, Putney, Vermont.

erty of the Corporation. The next year this contract was succeeded by a constitution, naming a president, secretary, and board of three directors. Among the earliest joiners was John R. Skinner, who later married Harriet Noyes, and John R. Miller who married Charlotte Noyes. Various other new members joined, a few seceded and a few were asked to leave. A lecture by Noyes—"Sexual Morality"—so outraged the populace of Putney by printing a tabu word (*sexuality*) that a church meeting was called in the town which passed a resolution that "perfectionism, as propagated by John H. Noyes, is a dangerous heresy." This was in 1847.

To inflame his enemies further, in that same year, at a meeting of believers at Putney on June 1, 1847, John Noyes made a momentous public declaration. "We believe that the Kingdom now coming is the same that was established in heaven at the Second Coming of Christ. Then God commenced a kingdom in human nature independent of the laws of this world. We look for

John Humphrey Noyes house, Putney, Vermont, where, in 1847, Central
Members of what later became the Oneida Community first drew together.
This house was built about the time of John Humphrey Noyes's marriage to
Harriet A. Holton, in 1838.

its reestablishment here, and this extension of an existing government into this world is that we mean by the kingdom of God. I
will put the question. Is not *now* the time for us to commence the
testimony that the Kingdom of God has come?"

According to the *Spiritual Magazine*, July 15, 1847, which
reported this meeting, "a discussion followed in which the nature
and effect of the proposed act were fully examined. All expressed
themselves deliberately and freely. It was seen that a new and further confession of truth was necessary. Therefore, it was unanimously adopted as the declaration of the believers assembled that
The Kingdom of God Has Come." Twenty-five years later, John
Humphrey Noyes wrote, "The declaration was made at an important crisis. It bore the same relation to the Oneida Community as
the Declaration of Independence did to the United States," as
George W. Noyes reported in *The Putney Community*.

The July 1, 1847, issue of the *Spiritual Magazine* following this triumphant declaration, opened with what sounded like a note of warning. "Nil medium! This was the motto of the Marquis of Montrose, a famous Scottish chieftain who fought and flourished two hundred years ago. It means, *No Half-way;* the whole or nothing. Whether it was his adherence to this principle in the stormy civil commotions of these days that finally brought his head to the block, we cannot say. But for those who enter the spiritual arena, the sooner they inscribe it on their banners and on their hearts, the better."

The July 15 issue of the *Spiritual Magazine* which actually contained the report of the June 1st meeting, made no further comment upon it but devoted most of its space to the case of Harriet Hall whom John Humphrey Noyes claimed to have cured by faith. This affair had raised a storm of opposition among the citizens of Putney, although Mrs. Hall and later her husband testified to the truth of the claim. One small item which appeared in this issue without comment was the announcement of the marriage of two couples who were members of the Putney Commune, which was supposed to have substituted their new form of Complex Marriage for the "fashions of this world." Whether this act was a sop to their more violent enemies, there is no way of knowing.

The issue for September 1 called attention to the forthcoming conventions at Genoa Five Corners and another at Lairdsville, both in New York State. The October 1 number gives detailed reports of both meetings which John Humphrey Noyes and his wife attended on September 3 and 17, respectively.

After a three-day session at Lairdsville, the principal resolution reached by the meeting was that its primary object was to facilitate acquaintance and promote union between the various Perfectionist groups. It is to be noted that certain names which appear in the history of the Oneida Community occur in the roll of those present at this meeting—Seymour, Ackley, Nash, Waters, Burt, Inslee and, of course, John and Harriet Noyes. The second convention, at Genoa, in Cayuga County, was a sort of continuation of that at Lairdsville, and many of the same names occur in the roll call. As Noyes reported it on October 1, 1847, "With great fervour, the strongest men of the convention came forward and pledged their lives, their fortunes and their sacred honor for the enterprise proposed and for the establishment of the Kingdom of God in the World."

The October 16 issue of the *Spiritual Magazine* opens with

a virulent attack on the Perfectionists' claim to faith healing, written by a local Methodist minister, the Reverend H. Eastman, followed by ten pages of rebuttal by John Noyes which closed with some bitterness: "We are struggling to gain a foothold for faith in a community where everyone inherits from his forefathers and drinks in with his mother's milk the spirit of the maxim that the age of miracles is past, and where all recognition of the agency of either God or the Devil in matters of health is scouted and scorned."

The November 23 issue contained nothing new or alarming —A Home Talk by John Humphrey Noyes, criticism of a popular demagogue who claimed to be in communication with the spirit of Swedenborg, various letters of testimony from distant adherents, and one brief note which some readers may have recognized as an inconspicuous gesture of farewell. "We find it convenient for the present to claim the ancient privilege of Perfectionist editors of issuing our paper at slightly irregular intervals. As it is not a newspaper, this circumstance will not affect its value or interest to subscribers. Without confining ourselves to exact dates, we shall expect to publish nearly twice a month, as heretofore."

Meanwhile in Putney public excitement against the prominent members of the Association had risen to a tumultuous pitch. What the *Spiritual Magazine* did not mention was that this rising uproar in Putney did not center at first upon the announced Kingdom of God or what the orthodox believed to be the licentious behavior of the members of the Association but on Noyes's claim to faith healing. The husbands of the two women whose cures had been claimed by Noyes rushed to the arms of the law, in this case the State's Attorney, and entered their complaints. In both cases these gentlemen repented their acts and signed retractions, but it was too late. The machinery of the law had been set in motion and on October 26 John Noyes was arrested. In view of the complaints as entered, it is strange that Noyes was arrested not for false or even blasphemous claims of having passed a miracle, but for adultery. Two thousand dollars bail was given by John R. Miller, the Association's treasurer, and Noyes was released on his own recognizance until trial, which was set for the following April.

As John's sister Harriet wrote to her mother (George W. Noyes, *Putney Community*) on October 29, 1847, "He was in duress about four hours and had opportunity to parry wit with the lawyers. He told them they would have first pickings of this affair, but that it was a controversy of principles and would have to be settled at last by priests and philosophers."

This was only the opening gun of the battle. It is not surprising that certain members of the Noyes family stood out against the Association. Horatio, John's younger brother, was an unreconcilable opponent, and his sister Mary and her husband, Larkin G. Mead, the lawyer to whom John had originally been articled, after wavering for a time, turned against him. Finally, Polly Hayes Noyes, the mother of the family, found it impossible to accept the authority of her own son at this time, although later, as she wrote in her *Recollections*, "It was a dark time for me but no sooner had Harriet [her daughter] opened her mouth and began to preach than the bubble burst and I was restored to my usual confidence."

These disputes were, of course, strictly within the family. The village outside was seething with excitement and, viewing this threat, Lawyer Mead sent for his brother-in-law and John Miller to come at once to Brattleboro. There he informed them that warrants for the arrest of John and Mary Cragin, two central members of the Association, were in the hands of the Sheriff.

In the discussion that followed, Mr. Mead recommended that all members of the Association not residents of Putney should leave the town at once and that John Noyes and the Cragins take flight for parts unknown. Though he must have recognized the seriousness of the situation, John Noyes was neither dismayed nor cast down and, as Miller afterwards reported, "It tried Mr. Mead exceedingly to see him feel so well in such circumstances."

Under Miller's guidance, the members departed variously for Connecticut, northern Vermont, and New York State, and, at two o'clock in the morning, the Cragins and their baby, with young William Hinds to drive them, left the commune. Noyes had already departed on foot for Boston. This was on November 26, 1847. Early in December, Noyes and Cragin joined forces in New York City.

Five years later, on April 4, 1852 (George W. Noyes, *The Putney Community*), John Noyes wrote Mead denying the charge that he had deserted his people to save his own skin:

> In the *Semi-weekly Eagle* I notice with some little protest a repetition of the old charge that I "absconded from Putney" and as you were a witness of all that I did, I have an inclination to note

down for your recollection the facts that will sometime come before the Court of public opinion.

1. I did not leave Putney on account of the arrest and bonds, but remained there a month after the law had taken possession of my case.

2. I was induced to go to Brattleboro finally not by fear of the law but by report from you and others that mob violence was impending.

3. I had no thought of leaving the state when I went to Brattleboro, but carried with me a written proposal to surrender myself to the custody of the law (without bail) on condition of peace for the rest of our family.

4. You and Mr. Bradley disapproved of my proposal and advised me to withdraw. I yielded to your advice as most likely to give peace.

5. Mr. Cragin and others "absconded" in like manner by my advice, or rather my explicit direction sent from Brattleboro with the approval of you and Mr. Bradley, and, as in my case, for the sake of peace.

The main point is that we left not to escape the law but to prevent an outbreak of lynch law among the barbarians of Putney.

It is worth remembering that the report from Brattleboro which set me in motion was that Dr. John Campbell had said, "If there is no law that will break them up, the people of Putney will make law for the occasion." This same Dr. Campbell had sometime previously committed an assault on Mr. Miller. Who, then, were the law abiders, and who were the law breakers? I was content to abide the issue and settle with the law as best I could. But Dr. John Campbell could not wait on the law, and he may thank his own turbulence that I escaped its clutches and saved him and his confederates from committing acts of disgraceful violence and perhaps murder.

George W. Noyes notes in *The Putney Community* that "at this crisis Noyes might easily have suffered martyrdom at the hands of a mob, as did Joseph Smith, the Mormon leader, three years before at Nauvoo, Illinois."

If, as John Noyes said and his associates believed, his aim was to promote peace in the village, peace certainly did not immediately follow his departure. Miller wrote him on November 27: "there is no mistake but what the move we have made was absolutely necessary. There was a great deal more excitement than I expected." Two days later he wrote, "There has been a perfect whirlwind of wrath and excitement since you left. . . . The people are determined to do all in their power to break up the corporation. They mean to push us till we divide all our property and live as the world lives." At a meeting, sixty citizens of Putney agreed on a Resolution in which, after detailing their grievances against the Association, its leaders, and its principles, they resolved that the moral interests of the village of Putney demanded the immediate dissolution of the Association, the immediate discontinuance of their magazine, and that those Perfectionists still remaining in town must publicly renounce those principles which tend to, and abandon those practices which are, a violation of the statute laws of the state. They added that "those citizens who had received serious injuries from the Association ought to be suitably remunerated by the Association." They required an answer in writing.

At first George Noyes and John Miller decided to attend the next meeting and give a public answer. Later, after a talk with Mr. Mead, who agreed to attend the meeting in their behalf, they waited until the committee called upon them. George, as his sister Harriet wrote to John Humphrey, was "almost crazy; said he could not live in that atmosphere," but the next day felt more cheerful. The townspeople, she had heard, inflamed themselves at their meetings but on the other hand they quarreled and she thought they would ultimately destroy themselves.

When the committee of citizens called at the Association they presented what Miller called "the most outrageous document ever written," asking the Perfectionists to admit that they had broken the laws of God and man and had become convinced of their error and promised to sign. The committee then demanded that they write a confession themselves, but George and John would only say "by word of mouth all they had to say," which was that nothing had been proved against them, but they would pledge themselves that in the future there would be nothing in their conduct which was a violation of the moral laws or the laws of the state.

The next day Miller wrote to Noyes that the trade at the store had got about as low as it could get—they traded twenty cents and made four cents profit. The smoke of battle, he added, had been so thick that it was almost impossible to see anything. Three days later he felt quite encouraged. Some of the townspeople had begun to speak in their favor, but on December 13, the Deputy Sheriff called with two writs against Noyes, for $3000 each and put an attachment on their real estate. At the next town meeting some of the youths of the town were "brawling against the speakers." A Vigilance Committee was appointed.

Perhaps in response to a note from his sister Harriet, begging him to "strengthen Mr. Miller and George. They almost stagger sometimes under the awful spirit they have to meet," John Noyes wrote his surrogates in Putney. He commended them and approved of the course they had taken during the crisis, agreed to the expediency of stopping the press temporarily and added that "if the pressure of Satan does not abate soon, I am perfectly willing that you should sell all our possessions in Putney. We have friends in all parts of the country who will be glad to give us refuge and help us to plant ourselves where we can grow with less molestation. As to acknowledging that we have done wrong, that is out of the question with me." He did apparently recognize that they might feel that they were suffering for his sake and reassured them that he would not "brave public opinion unnecessarily and shall have an eye to the bearings of my proceedings on your position." He added in closing, "It seems hardly right that I should be free and comfortable while you are battling with the storms of Putney. But then I thought that my presence with you would only increase the fury of the storm, and that it would do you no good to see me imprisoned or assassinated."

If he saw this letter, Lawyer Mead was not appeased. "It is intended," he wrote Miller, "to prosecute the male members of your Corporation for gross lewdness or some other offense against chastity, morality and decency." As for John in New York, he wrote ominously, "as soon as it is discovered that he is carrying on his principles there (and he is watched there) he will be transferred from his pleasant parlour to a less pleasant tenement in the City Prison."

On Christmas Day, Miller reported that he had just received an anonymous letter warning him that he would be tarred and feathered and ridden on a rail if he did not leave town immediately, but although he admitted that they had had "some rather hard pinches," they were doing well. Mr. Mead and his wife Mary came to visit them and Mary said that John thought he had been raised up to introduce his doctrine into the world, but she thought *she* was raised up to put a stop to it. Brother Horatio declared that Young George would not live three months as a result of these trials, but their sister Charlotte wrote that "George sees a direct connection between our faith and the tree of life, and is renewing his strength."

Three months before these violent happenings, one of the resolutions recorded by the Genoa Convention in September had declared "that it is expedient to take measures immediately for forming a heavenly Association in Central New York." This, obediently, a handful of converts—Jonathan Burt, Joseph Ackley, Daniel Nash, William Hatch and others—did in November of that year. As soon as they were somewhat settled and in running order, they invited John Humphrey Noyes to visit them.

On January 20, 1848, Noyes wrote his wife from New York: "A new door is opening for us. When I think how opportunely you and I went west and started the Association movement, and how the Spirit and Providence of God have followed in the track of the plan which I proposed for concentrating on Oneida, I am ready to imagine that God has been preparing to transplant us from Putney as he transplanted the gospel from New Haven at the beginning. I have determined to go to Oneida and see what can be done there." He would have preferred to leave a foothold in Putney and one in New York City, but "that would be leaving a hostile fortress in our rear, which is contrary to the rules of strategy. Our better way will be to make a lateral movement and join our friends at Oneida."

On the invitation of Burt, Mr. Noyes visited Oneida, and "as a result of these negotiations, on the 1st of February, 1848, the present Association was commenced by a full union between J. H. Noyes and J. Burt, and a transfer of $500 of U.S. stock, by J. H. Noyes to the stock of the new Union." The Kingdom of God, as the Genoa Resolution ordained, now had an external manifestation.

Early in February Noyes wrote from Oneida to George Cragin at Putney that "everything conspires to bring about a concentration. I have the enthusiastic confidence of all now on the ground." The accommodations, he admitted, would be primitive: for the Cragins, "a small house with one comfortable room, with buttery, a back kitchen for summer, a bedroom upstairs, a good barn, a small shoemaker's shop and twenty-three acres of land. I think you can live at least as comfortably there with your children as the Beaver Meadow folks [the three families who had originally joined Mr. Burt at Oneida in November] live in their shanty. (And I assure you they are happy) until we can build a Chateau. Hatch [a Beaver Meadow man] says, 'the King Bee has lit and the swarm is coming,' and truly it seems so. Prospects open rich, though for the present we must make up our minds for soldiers' fare. We have good luck in everything so far and I feel that the divine energy is pushing us forward, and therefore I feel safe in an adventurous course."

By February Harriet had written her approval of the move, and Noyes wrote Cragin minute directions for bringing the whole Putney group by train, to arrive at Oneida on March 1. When the refugees arrived—seventeen adults and their children—the available accommodations could hardly be called comfortable. Their first enterprise was the building of a communal home.

During the rest of that year and the next, 1849, when the *First Annual Report* was published, the farm was worked and the sawmill was run, but the income from these sources could not be expected to meet the expenses of the Association which then, and for some years to come, depended upon the capital brought in by joining members plus the subsidies furnished by outside friends. The communists were not depressed by this situation but considered this period as "properly and necessarily one of preparation and outlay. The opportunities and prospects for profitable business in lumbering and several kinds of manufacture already commenced or contemplated are very good and it is not unreasonable to expect that after the present season of necessary preparation, it will become a self-supporting institution."

The Kingdom of God was established and in business.

The history of perfectionism, the religious movement that culminated in the teachings of John Humphrey Noyes and the founding of the Oneida Community, as given in their *First Annual Report*, is succinct but perhaps insufficiently informative for the modern reader. "In February, 1834, John H. Noyes began to preach the doctrine of perfect holiness and other kindred 'heresies,' and laid the foundation of what in 1834 was called the school of modern Perfectionism." The missing fact here is that what they called "modern Perfectionism" in 1834 was not the original creation of John Noyes.

Previous to this time, as his nephew G. W. Noyes wrote in *The Religious Experience of John Humphrey Noyes*, "The doc-

John Humphrey Noyes, around 1851.

trine of Christian perfection had been taught by a number of revival leaders, notably James Latourette, John B. Foot, and Hiram
Sheldon. During the period of religious enthusiasm in the early
thirties, these men had gained a considerable following, especially
in the State of New York. The New York Perfectionists, as they
were called, were all Wesleyan in their original characteristics."

As John Noyes wrote of them, "New York Perfectionism
and New Haven Perfectionism may be regarded as twin products

of the great revival which stirred the heart of the American Nation in the forepart of the 19th Century. New York Perfectionism was the elder by a few months and, like Esau, was wild and barbaric; while New Haven Perfectionism was more intellectual and civilized." Latourette, whom Noyes later referred to as "the emperor of Perfectionism," began to preach to a congregation in New York City in the early 1830s. His immediate converts were drawn from the vicinity of New York City and Newark, New Jersey, which thus became the primary distributing centers of New York Perfectionism.

Upstate New York, particularly the central counties, were then what has been called "The Burnt-over District," a region widely converted by the recent Finney revivals. At Delphi, New York, Sheldon and a few associates began a Perfectionist movement in 1833, and at about the same time, another group, stemming from the New York City colony, was established at Albany under the leadership of John B. Foot and two sisters by the name of Annsley. As George W. Noyes writes, "This Albany group proved to be exceedingly virile and became even more important as a distributing center than its parent colony. During 1832 and 1833, missionaries went in every direction and numerous Perfectionist colonies sprang up."

One of these missionaries wrote to James Boyle, a member of The Free Church of New Haven, who with Noyes was then (1834-35) publishing a magazine entitled *The Perfectionist.* "I have been recently in Owasco preaching Christ a Savior from sin. I attended a meeting held in an orchard. An immense concourse of people were present—one or two thousand from fifteen or twenty miles about." Another letter from Genoa, New York, speaks of "visiting the saints in DeRuyter, Delphi, Cazenovia, Smithfield, Augusta, Verona, Chittenango, Canastota, Manlius, Salina, etc. At Canastota, being sent for, Brothers Randall, Hatch and myself held a 'preach' upon one of the [Erie] Canal Bridges to a full congregation."

Not only in these widely differing branches of Perfectionism but in a dozen other newly invented religious groups, Free Love, so-called, was openly advocated, along with freedom in practically everything else. Affinities, counterparts, spiritual wives, Swedenborg and his concubines, Thomas Lake Harris and his "divine respiration and chastity in true nuptial union," the Brimfield Bundling, Lovett's "spiritual mating," these and many other variations on the sexual theme were practiced, especially throughout New England and Western New York State in the "Burnt-over District."

Back as far as the foreign-born Rappites and Zoarites, marriage, though tolerated, was looked upon with disfavor. Robert Owen merely included it as one of the "awful trinity of man's oppressors," but his son, Robert Dale Owen, "was outspoken in his enmity to marriage and became a leading advocate of free divorce," as George W. Noyes noted in *Putney Community*.

The Mormon version—polygamy—John Noyes called "a dilution of marriage" and Josiah Warren, the inventor of "Individual Sovereignty," encouraged free love in his community, Modern Times. The well-known Stephen Pearl Andrews joined a water-cure specialist, Dr. Thomas Nichols, in establishing a Free Love School at Port Chester, New York, in 1852 and published a *Journal* and several books on the subject. George W. Noyes wrote in *Putney Community:* "So widespread was the popularity of these new doctrines that Dr. Nichols ventured upon overt acts in the full glare of publicity. With his partner he instituted a series of 'Sociables' in New York City which were broken up by the police." After this, since Spiritualism was a part of Nichols' doctrine —the "spirits" helped him to write his books—he formed a "Protective Union" with a Central Bureau where "all who wished to associate were enrolled as members and received a printed list of names and addresses for affinity hunters."

Later, at Berlin Heights in Ohio, Nichols' western disciples formed a commune whose publication, *The Social Revolutionist*, became the organ of "fierce Spiritualistic Free Lovers." Unfortunately, the local public was inflamed to the point of seizing and burning the paper by a mob, after which the remaining members fell into disarray. There were several suicides, one member was thrown into prison, and three-quarters of the married couples separated. In 1874 nine former members of the Berlin Heights group applied for membership and were received in the Oneida Community, to its ultimate regret. Strangely enough, after the collapse of another of Nichols' communes, "Harmonic Home" at Yellow Springs, Ohio, the doctor and his wife seem to have given up hope of social reconstruction and, recanting their errors, were received into the Roman Catholic Church.

Certain of the scattered groups which identified themselves as Perfectionists, encountered a stumbling block in the form of

Antinomianism: "the assumption of freedom from the external law of spoken or written statutes, while not yet under the internal law of heart and mind," George W. Noyes wrote in *Religious Experience*, "takes different forms according to the temperamental susceptibilities of its subjects. In those inclined to sensuality, it takes the form of lasciviousness; in those whose leading trait is self-esteem, the form of anti-organization; in those of an indolent disposition, the form of passivism."

The Brimfield Bundling was a somewhat orgiastic affair which took place at Brimfield, Massachusetts, in March 1835. The members of the Perfectionist group there had for sometime been encouraging "a seducing tendency of freedom of manners between the sexes. The expressions "Dearly Beloved," "brother," and "sister" were in common use, and kissing between members was equally free. John Noyes visited these brethren, but, after an enthusiastic goodnight kiss from one of the young women, he "got a clear view of the situation and received what he believed to be an order to withdraw." He departed alone and took a bee-line on foot in zero weather for Putney. But Dr. Gridley, of Southampton, boldly espoused the movement of "gospel liberty," and, wrote G. W. Noyes, "for years his house was the scene of scandalous practices, in which he took a leading part."

Theophilus R. Gates, the publisher of a paper in Philadelphia called *The Reformer and Christian*, was first introduced to the New Haven Perfectionists by John B. Foot and Chauncey Dutton. Anti-organization had been Gates's hobby for more than twenty years. "The true love of God in the heart is the best restraint, and a tender conscience is the best discipline," was his doctrine, according to Robert Allerton Parker, in *A Yankee Saint*.

After Noyes had separated from Boyle and the paper *Perfectionist*, in January 1835, Gates rapidly became intimate with Boyle and Charles Weld (another adversary of Noyes's). After this Noyes's writings no longer appeared in the *Perfectionist* and instead Gates's sermons took the post of honor.

This new apostle wrote in the *Perfectionist* for February 1835, "All sectarianism is the work of carnal men." In the May 20 issue, "We entertain no predilection for the name 'Perfectionist.'" Again, "We are certain that all sects and sectarian names will ere long be utterly destroyed." As Dutton, another of Boyle's adherents, wrote to Noyes in April 1835 (*Religious Experience*, George

W. Noyes): "I have done receiving anything from the Bible, or from the hand of man. Nothing abides when the storm comes but what the Lord has taught."

The next step was Gates's rejection of the teachings of the Apostle Paul who, as a human teacher, could be impeached as one "who was taught of God." Finally Gates indicted not only Paul but the other Apostles. To Gates's anti-organizationism was added the passivism of Boyle & Co. which declared that there was too much "leaning on the paper" *(The Perfectionist).* One eager convert to this new theory wrote, "Cursed is he that maketh the arm of flesh his trust; It seems to me that the paper does not point distinctly enough at Jesus." Since Boyle himself had come to agree that this carnal arm was superfluous, the paper was discontinued without notice in March, 1836.

As a young man, Theophilus Gates had taught school unsuccessfully in a number of places until, after experiencing conversion, he declared that the Lord required him to preach the gospel to others. This he did as a traveling evangelist, rebuking his hearers for their unchristian ways and uttering dire prophecies of the end of the Turkish Empire and with it all the nations of Europe, ending in "one of the most awful and sanguinary contests ever recorded on the pages of history." The date set for these dreadful events was 1833, and when that time passed without any alarming occurrences, he said naively, in *The Witness,* June 6, 1840, that he had only expressed his honest belief.

John Noyes's comment on this failure was merely that Gates had followed his own interpretations and not the mind of the Lord. However, Gates's impeachment of the Apostle Paul, in his publication *The Reformer and Christian,* was a heresy which outraged John Noyes, whose especial hero was Paul. In *The Witness,* a paper which Noyes began to issue in 1840, Noyes wrote that Gates "not only speaks in general terms of Paul's not having attained to perfect righteousness but even speaks of him and the other apostles as being, in a measure, thieves and robbers."

From this and a number of other references to Gates that appear in *The Witness,* it seems obvious that the two prophets were exceedingly antagonistic, which may explain the mix-up—if it was really a mix-up—in the publication of what came to be known as the *Battle Ax* letter.

It all began with a letter written by John Humphrey Noyes to one of his most devoted adherents, David Harrison of Meriden,

Connecticut, on January 1, 1837. Eight months later, this letter appeared, unheralded and unsigned, in T. R. Gates's new periodical, *The Battle Ax and Weapons of War*, in August 1837, with an introduction by Mr. Gates himself.

"The following extract of a letter is from a person of liberal education who was a preacher in the Presbyterian or Congregational Church, and who stood foremost among the Perfectionists at New Haven, when they first came forth in the light and power of a better state of things. The open and undisguised manner in which he has expressed himself in the close of the extract on a very important subject, the uprightness and purity of his intentions and the sacrifice I know he has made, from principle, demand of the reader a candid hearing."

Extracts from the letter which was dated January 15, 1837:

> I call a certain woman my wife—she is yours, she is Christ's and in him she is the bride of all saints. She is dear in the hand of a stranger, and according to my promise to her, I rejoice. My claim on her cuts directly across the marriage vows of this world and God knows the end.
>
> When the will of God is done on earth as it is in heaven, *there will be no more marriage*. The marriage supper of the Lamb is a feast at which *every dish is free to every guest*. Exclusiveness, jealousy, quarreling, have no place there, for the same reason as that which forbids the guests at a thanksgiving dinner to claim each his separate dish and quarrel with the rest for his right. In a holy community there is no more reason why sexual intercourse should be restrained by law than why eating and drinking should be—and there is as little occasion for shame in the one case as in the other.

Gates added, "The letter from which the preceding extracts are made, having been sent to me by another hand than the writer's, I have withheld the name, though satisfied he would have no objection for it to appear."

In *The Witness* of the next month, September 1837, John Noyes published an acknowledgment of authorship: "Several persons have written to inquire whether I or Mr. Boyle was the author of a letter lately published in the *Battle Ax*. I answer, I am the author, *but not the publisher* of the letter. As an anti-mason, I cannot object to its publication; and as an optimist, I am bound to rejoice. Yet I must be permitted to say that it contains doctrines and allusions which I should never have obtruded upon the public, not from fear of persecution or reproach but lest my liberty should become a stumbling-block to others. Since it is published, it is proper that I should acknowledge myself its author."

This was by no means all of the innocent mix-up, if indeed it was innocent. Letters apparently poured in to the publisher of the now-famous letter.

A letter from Noyes dated May 15, 1838, from Ithaca, New York, carried in *The Witness*, January 23, 1839, made explicit the whole affair:

> Several mistakes have been made by the public about the *Battle Ax* Letter, which I will correct for you and you may correct them for the public or not, as you please.
> (1) That letter was written not to T. R. Gates but to David Harrison of Meriden, Conn.
> (2) The latter was written not for the public but for the perusal of a familiar friend, with due regard to the delicacy of the subject and without any intention of obtruding it upon the notice even of the Perfectionists—much less of casting it before dogs and swine. Evidence of this may be found in the letter itself.

The mechanics of the whole fraud were disclosed in a letter from David Harrison, which Noyes appended to his letter to Garrison.

> I have never told you how the *Battle Ax* letter escaped me. I kept it several months without showing it to anyone; but the Lord gave me no liberty to suppress it. I first showed it to Lovett—he liked it and wished to peruse it—I consented but requested him to return it. While it was with him, Elizabeth Hawley got hold of it and insisted on sending it to Gates or "she would leave the house in a thunderstorm that night for New Haven." So it went. I soon heard of it and anticipated the result but should have written immediately to Gates, forbidding its publication, but I could not get the Lord's consent. So, you see, the Lord obtained the letter from me, as it were, by stealth.
> [signed] David Harrison.

All this would sound like a tempest in a very small theological teapot except for the repercussions it made on the many

Elizabeth Hawley was instrumental in
transmitting the famous *Battle Ax*
letter to Theophilus Gates in 1837.

and various free-thinking groups about the country. Theophilus
Gates, having stolen and appropriated for himself the thunder of
the *Battle Ax* letter, now established himself as the head and front
of the freest of the Free Love cults, and Gatesism became a potent
word. *The Witness,* Noyes's paper, published occasional reports of
the doings of the Gatesites.

The fact that Gates had, as it were, pirated Noyes's idea
and applied it—out of context—to antinomianism was infuriating
to Noyes. He had Harrison write Gates to demand the return of
the original letter. Gates obliged, accompanying it with a bland
note carried in *The Witness* of December 30, 1840, which rallied
Harrison about "being so scared before he was hurt" and called
him—and Noyes by inference—"indeed children for whom allow-
ance must be made. He had supposed that Noyes would rejoice to

see the promulgation of his honest views." He said that he and his people were prepared to lay down their lives in support of life principles. He advised them that he was about to reprint the second number of the *Battle Ax* and, "should I do so, I expect to *leave out Mr. Noyes's letter part.*"

The famous letter appeared in the reprinted second number of the *Battle Ax* and was accompanied by an address to its readers thus: "In republishing this number I shall leave out the greater part of an extract of a letter inserted in the first edition, except for a few words below."

The "few words," as Noyes noted in *The Witness*, December 30, 1840, "included *all that part of it relating to marriage which has been matter of complaint and offense*, and leaves out all that part relating to faith and patience which has generally been regarded as the redeeming part of the letter. By *pretending* to leave out my letter, he acknowledges his obligation to rectify a wrong, and by *actually retaining* it, he makes himself a bare-faced transgressor of that obligation. The question in this case is, *whether T. R. Gates is not a liar?* I submit it to the jury without argument."

One special note appended to this outburst is certainly understandable in view of the situation but it does smack a little of special pleading. "N.B. In consequence of my apparent association with Gates, and other circumstances beyond my control, my sentiments in relation to marriage, the liberty of the sexes . . . have been so misunderstood and misrepresented that not only have the adversaries of holiness had an occasion of evil surmising and evil speaking—but some, I have reason to believe, who profess to be saved from sin have thought of me as though 'I have walked after the flesh,' and have corrupted themselves with doctrines of licentiousness, thinking that therein they had my countenance and fellowship."

In this article, he added, "In consequence of this forgery, I lost many friends and gained many enemies." He might perhaps be forgiven some bitterness, since at that time he had just attempted to launch his own publication, *The Witness*, in Ithaca, New York, and this loss of friends—and subscribers—left him practically bankrupt. He was obliged to abandon the project at least temporarily and for the rest of the winter of 1837-38 he stayed with Abram Smith, an enthusiastic proselyte, who had a farm in the little village of Rondout, just across the Hudson River from Kingston, New York.

Smith had been a vigorous member of a coterie of Perfectionists in New Haven which included Mr. and Mrs. Lyvere, James Boyle, Charles Weld and Smith's wife, Mary Ann. At that time John Noyes was also a member, but after his falling-out with Boyle in 1836 and the incursion of Theophilus Gates, plus Noyes's letter condemning Weld and all his works, the group was broken up into three parties: the legalist party who were members of the Free Church; the Antinomian party under Weld and Gates, and a middle party led by Smith, who still claimed to be a disciple of Noyes.

The party under Weld and Gates had migrated from New Haven to New York City, Newark, New Jersey, and farther south. Gates, who by this time was the dominant member, moved to Philadelphia where he preached—and practiced—his new gospel which had now discarded all rules, all leaders, all regular meetings and "needed only to be taught of God" largely by spirit messages, dreams, impressions, and impulses. Naturally Noyes's disclaimer in *The Witness* article was utterly ignored by these radicals.

This article was published in the number of *The Witness* dated December 30, 1840, a date particularly interesting for two reasons. First it admits as a fact that the so-called *Battle Ax* doctrine—promulgated by Gates, it is true, but even more widely known as the conception of John Humphrey Noyes—had gained adherents not only among the saved and sinless but among the libertarians and antinomians. And secondly, it came at the end of a personal conflict between Noyes and his "strong right arm," Abram Smith, and it involved two of his most recent converts.

The story of this involvement, told by itself, would seem no more than a shocking or scandalous anecdote of adultery and faithlessness set against a prim and straight-laced Victorian background. Actually, in the circles in which these protagonists moved —radical free-thinkers, rebels against convention—such behavior was the rule rather than the exception. In a feverishly religious age, these people rejected orthodox religion and worldly convention and substituted a dozen strange and permissive doctines of their own invention, which is not to say that many of these believers were not sincerely, even passionately devoted to their various exotic creeds. In the example given, two, at least, of the actors in the drama were unquestionably believers. If there were also hypocrites and charlatans, that is perhaps no more than can be said of every deception since Adam and Eve and the Serpent. In this case, at least, two of the actors repented and reformed.

THE CRAGINS

JUST AS A SILHOUETTE—stark black against pure white—holds the eye almost hypnotically, printing its outline upon the retina of the beholder, by the same token in a canvas or a tapestry, where design flows into design, the beholder is apt to turn away with no clear impression of what he has seen. In the same way an event witnessed alone, perhaps a criminal act like a murder committed in an empty street, would make an unforgettable impression upon a sole witness, every word spoken, every motion of the criminal or the victim would be printed upon the memory of the observer. On the other hand, that same act, performed in the midst of an excited, hurrying, pressing crowd or in a battle, might even escape notice altogether.

Marriage and divorcement, love affairs and adultery have always been good for whispered scandal, even in the most straight-laced society. In a period when social behavior had been confused, not to say corrupted, by the introduction of a dozen new and alarming so-called religions, even the most scabrous details of yet another piece of brazen misconduct may draw no more than the most casual attention.

Utopia, or, as the religionists said, the Kingdom of Heaven, was to be won only by those following an approved code of behavior—celibacy or marriage, Shakers or Quakers, Millennialists or Second Adventists, Millerites or Spiritualists, Swedenborgians or Oneida Perfectionists, differed as widely as possible in their philosophies. Perhaps the point of hottest debate in the middle of the last century concerned, pro and con, celibacy versus Free Love, under whatever name the adversaries chose to call it.

And the episode which excited disapproval in certain of the followers of these leaders was scarcely more than a commonplace to the armies of devotees on either side of the fence. The actors in this small drama were recent converts to the Perfectionism preached by John Humphrey Noyes. They were George Cragin and his wife, Mary, both born of prosperous New England families —he from Massachusetts and she from Maine—who had met, married, and lived for a time in New York City. Viewed against the background of bizarre social and sexual theories being expounded and experiments being actually tried at that time, their experience seems neither remarkable nor incredible. They were the children of their age, both being by nature believers, perhaps fanatics, and it is possible that if they had happened to fall under the influence not of Noyes but of one or another of the contemporary spellbinders, their history would have been equally anomalous.

We have a good deal of explicit information about George since he wrote and published in the Oneida Community *Circular* from February 18, 1865, to May 7, 1866, a serial autobiography entitled *The Story of a Life.* It is detailed, solemn, somewhat pompous, and probably truthful, as it was given him to see the truth about himself and his life.

He told the story with great simplicity. Because of the failure of his father's business he had only a minimal education but was put to work, first in Boston and then in New York, in the wholesale grocery business at a salary of one hundred and fifty dollars a year. How he managed to live on this sum, even in the 1830s, is not disclosed. His employer he describes as a "Merchant prince." Himself, he admits, was a country boy, naive and impressionable, willing to believe whatever he was told and naturally attracted to the fair sex. He mentions a Jane, a Sarah, an Emily, ladies who devoted themselves to rescuing "fallen women" and, he admits, even the "fallen women" themselves called forth his interest and compassion.

George had been from boyhood of a religious turn, and in his first year away from home he joined the multitude of converts of Charles G. Finney, one of the most effective evangelists of that period. Young George became a member of Finney's Tabernacle Church as teacher of a class in his Sabbath school and it was through this connection that he met, fell in love with, and eventually married Miss Mary Johnson who, at that time, was teaching an infant school of nearly two hundred pupils.

His first description of her was as "a beautiful, smiling face," but he cautiously adds—in parenthesis—"(whoever saw a smiling face that was not beautiful?)" Mary had been engaged at that moment in searching for one of her charges whose parents had apparently abandoned it. George, as he writes, his "benevolence acting in concert with my admiration for female loveliness, needed no spur to make me volunteer to help her." After that she could do no less than ask him to her home to meet her family.

Although later, after their marriage, George confesses to a love for his wife almost amounting to idolatry, at this earlier time he remarks with his usual caution that "although there were perturbations and commotions in the region of my solar plexus by so near approach of a brilliant luminary, it must not be inferred however, that Miss Johnson possessed anything more than ordinary intellectual powers. Her strength, talent and tact were to be found in her social, affectional and religious nature rather than in her intellectual."

Whether this unflattering analysis was right or wrong, George, in his pious way, had been quite a beau, susceptible to the charms of a number of young ladies, but one day, on parting with Mary he found that a queer sensation passed over him, as though he had parted with a large share of himself and later, during a short walk, in spite of the charms of one of his other lady friends, "Miss Johnson's personal attractiveness served to intoxicate my social nature to some extent." By this time he was so far gone in what he called "the delicious mire of falling in love" that the sight of Mary on the arm of another escort made him admit to himself that he was "under the exciting influence of the green-eyed monster."

There could be but one outcome of this romance. Mary was obliged to go away for a month, and during that time George made his proposal by mail. Mary's reply—a refusal—dashed his ardor for only a moment. She had declined to marry him because her father, as George had perhaps noticed, after the failure of his business had become a drunkard. This was no deterrent to George, whose own father had gone the same sad way. When Mary returned, to use George's elegant language, he "gave Miss Johnson to understand that I had no intention whatever of countermanding the request for her hand in marriage and I had her hand in mine when the affirmative yes, was given and sealed on those sweet lips with a kiss which, I must aver, was the first salutation of that kind that I had ever given woman."

For the next few months, aside from an occasional lovers' quarrel and a few difficulties with some of George's lady friends, everything went smoothly. The knot was finally tied on February 7, 1834, and after "congratulations and cakes and wine," the newlyweds were "whirled off in a mail coach to honeymoon in Newark, New Jersey."

The story of the next few years shifts from the dramatic to the connubial and domestic. Of their married life, George admits that it "savored too much of creature idolatry. We were childishly and unwisely absorbed in the intimacy offered us by the marriage relation," and Mary's health began to suffer until a doctor advised that they room apart for three months. The only other difficulty was that Mary confessed that she had no experience in the usual duties of housekeeping; she did not even know how to make bread, or to cook in general, although she was willing to learn. Her new husband forgave her and promised to teach her.

Financially too, there were disappointments. George and two young friends went into partnership in a wholesale commission business but after a few months of hard going the young friends lost heart and all three agreed to give up the enterprise. Another jobbing house offered George a position as agent, to go to Europe as a buyer, but he declined on the grounds that he must give up either his mercantile career or his religion, since his would-be employer was an infidel. Mary apparently concurred, although at that time their first child had just been born and they needed money. However, the baby did not survive. At this time there was no revenue coming in and George was obliged to admit that this state of things could not long continue without "creating a miniature national debt, to which he was decidedly opposed."

Fortunately, a group of ladies, known as the Female Moral Reform Society, warm admirers—and backers—of a popular Moral Reformer named McDowall, had undertaken to publish a paper called, naturally, *The Advocate of Moral Reform*. It appeared that Mr. McDowall, however talented at rescuing brands from the burning, was no accountant. "Charges were trumped up against him for squandering funds," George Cragin wrote. "He was sensitive and became disheartened." The situation as business manager of *The Advocate* was offered to George and he accepted gladly, the only drawback being that he was occasionally obliged to travel. This was a great cross to him. "For more than a year I had not been absent from my wife for twenty-four hours. Now I might possibly be separated from her for two or three weeks. On taking leave of her the childish feelings of my nature got the better of my manhood, causing sobs and tears to manifest themselves in place of smiles and manly courage." In view of the tribulations he was to suffer later, one cannot but be sympathetic with poor George.

In the spring of 1839 the Cragins became acquainted with a number of Perfectionists, most of them followers of J. B. Lyvere and Abram C. Smith with whom John Noyes had been associated two years before. As George Cragin reports it in *Story of a Life:* "They were mostly poor and illiterate and without an influence in society," which seems a curious commentary from a future communist. However, he candidly admits the reason for it: "I was probably jealous of their influence upon Mrs. Cragin who would gladly have sat at the feet of a street beggar if she could have obtained the living water that alone can nourish the thirsty soul."

By the autumn, Mary had "gone through the conflict, counted the cost of being cast out of society, rejected and disowned by relatives, so great was the odium cast upon the so-called heresy, Perfectionism." After an equally severe struggle, George followed suit. As Mary wrote on November 22, 1839, to J. H. Noyes, "It is now nearly four weeks since I was translated from the kingdom of darkness: and, weeping for joy," she adds that "one week since, my dear husband entered the kingdom."

The news of this translation soon spread among their acquaintances, and shortly the ladies of the Moral Reform Society, for whom George worked, called him before a special board meeting where he was closely questioned, especially about the *Battle Ax* letter, and when he refused to denounce Mr. Noyes as a deceiver and a bad man, he was dismissed from their service.

After this, since they were now abandoned by most of their earlier friends and George was without a job, the outcasts turned to the group of Perfectionists in the city among whom Lyvere and Abram Smith were regarded as the most advanced. Mr. Smith, although he lived at Roundout, seventy-five miles up the North River, was in New York so frequently that they "had the pleasure of seeing him nearly as much as we did those who resided in the city." Mr. and Mrs. William Green, lately of the Moral

Reform Group, had "handsome property in New Jersey" where the Cragins hoped, on communistic principles, to obtain asylum in their hour of need.

With the rest of the group, unorganized and unregulated, George found it difficult to sympathize. The one ordinance they respected, apparently, was salutation by a kiss, but George did not enjoy this. "All must be loved alike and treated alike if we would be impartial. To conform to such a rule, I had a decided inability and after a while refused to kiss a person simply for forms sake," an attitude which troubled his conscience and brought down upon him the frowns and censures of his new friends.

Mary, naturally out-going and uncritical, had no such inhibitions; her house "became a place of rendezvous for Perfectionists generally and she became a very popular member of the fraternity," receiving rather more attention from some of the brotherhood than suited George's taste, which naturally resulted in George's becoming an unpopular member of the circle.

The first step in the painful road George Cragin was to travel came with an invitation from Abram Smith to accompany him to the funeral of one of the members of the group, which was to take place at the handsome estate of Mr. and Mrs. Green in New Jersey. Mrs. Green had been George's employer on *The Advocate of Moral Reform* until she and her husband suddenly converted to Perfectionism. With this association in mind, it must have been a shock to George, during the two days while the funeral party was snow-bound at Mr. Green's house, to observe "much unedifying talk and loose behavior."

Whether John Noyes was there we do not know, but in view of his disapproval of such antinomian antics, it seems unlikely, though he must have heard of it, for he noted severely that "there was great wantonness" on this occasion. Even the host, Mr. Green, did not join the fun and afterwards rejected not only his wanton guests but ultimately renounced Perfectionism, along with Noyes and all his works, reacting as far as Shakerism. George Cragin's comment thirty years later was "that one thing was certain—we were sheep without a shepherd and were surrounded by beasts of prey."

The man from whom they looked for help was Abram Smith, whose right to a superior position in the new group was based upon his claim of "unity and partnership with Mr. J. H. Noyes." As George Cragin wrote, "we accepted Mr. Smith as an under-teacher whom, we were led to infer, the superior had appointed." Smith, who had associated with them often in the New York group, now brought his wife, Mary Ann, to call upon them, and at this time both of the Smiths invited the Cragins to join their family at Rondout. Mary Ann was introduced as a newly made convert but despite "her smiles and winning ways," George was not favorably impressed. However, since the expected invitation from the Greens did not materialize, Smith's invitation seemed the only alternative.

Oddly enough, since George was completely devoted to Smith, "as a son to a father," it was Mary, usually so credulous, who had misgivings about the move to Rondout. Nevertheless, since it was necessary to move somewhere, move they must and did in March 1840, although Mary was so apprehensive that her feelings found vent in a flood of tears and as she later told her husband, from that moment "darkness like an impenetrable cloud came over her mind."

They both found the Smith family, in residence, something of a shock. The pre-Revolutionary stone house, on the bank of a creek opposite the village of Rondout, was so sparsely furnished that they were obliged to conclude that one of Smith's virtues was economy carried to the point of parsimony. This was the least of their new troubles. Mr. Smith's real business, he explained, was as foreman of a lime manufacturing plant across the river in Kingston. He had neither time nor interest in the farm which he rented from a brother-in-law. Mr. Cragin, fortunately, was delighted to assume this responsibility and spent long hours of work on the farm. "Possessing communistic ideas," George wrote later, "we thus made a slight attempt to carry out the Pentecostal spirit of holding all things in common. This suited Mr. Smith, as he had earned the reputation of keeping those under him pretty constantly employed," and George "very soon became much absorbed in his new avocation."

In the spring after the somewhat orgiastic funeral, Smith had had a clash with William Green and brought back some of the "liberty views" of the New York group to his household at Rondout. There Mary Cragin, a natural enthusiast, received them joyfully and wrote to John Noyes of the "glorious fires" in the Smith family, since she had emerged from the cloud of Shakerism under which she had apparently been led by the volatile Mr. Green.

In spite of the "glorious fires," the situation at Rondout

was becoming extremely uncomfortable. After the arrival of the Cragins in her home, Mary Ann Smith developed a violent antagonism to her husband, and presently the Smiths were at each other's throats. There may have been some reason for this enmity. As George Cragin naively noted, there was now a certain coolness between himself and Abram Smith, but "on the other hand, Smith's communications with Mrs. Cragin were more frequent and more private."

"Did I discover," wrote guileless George, a "corresponding coolness on the part of Mrs. Cragin? She had little to say to me except in criticism of a spirit in me which claimed her affections."

Both he and Mary still believed with John Noyes that possessive "special" love was of the devil. Freely and sincerely did George admit that, in forsaking all for Christ, his wife was included. Between an accusing conscience and an idolatrous love for his wife it seemed as though the more he struggled the deeper he sank into despair.

Matters worsened in the old stone house. By the first of May, Smith turned his wife out of her home, to take refuge across the creek with her relatives. In his own home he, as religious teacher and surrogate for John Noyes, instructed Mary Cragin how to proceed. George, who had been set to work long hours a day ploughing the farm behind a blind horse, was too exhausted to object. Abram told Mary to feign distress of mind in the night and "repair to his chamber for spiritual relief." ("My God," Cragin prayed, "Is this necessary to cure me of the marriage spirit?") The routine was established until, like a direct answer to prayer, Noyes and two of his cohorts, David Harrison and John Skinner, appeared at their door.

This was an interruption, but for the moment Smith actually welcomed it, since the townspeople of Rondout, aroused by the infuriated Mary Ann, got out a warrant against Smith for breach of the peace, and the town hoodlums were planning to attack. Although Smith was willing to fight, Noyes counseled peace with the outside world and criticism at home. He investigated the situation, rebuking Smith and Mary for their behavior, and "admonished them faithfully but in love." Cragin, a glutton for punishment, joined in denouncing his own legality and forgave Smith and Mary, considering himself equally sinful with them. That evening Noyes left for Putney, taking Smith with him, and the mob was satisfied.

Smith's visit to Putney in the role of a repentant sinner must have been a masterpiece of blandishment since after a fortnight he returned to Rondout to assure the amenable Mary that Noyes had really approved of their recent affair, had only criticized them for the benefit of George, and that in Putney, Smith reported, he had discussed the whole thing with their leader and had received his complete approval. George, loaded down with hard work and self-condemnation, was too absorbed in trying to win the justification and peace of Christ to notice what was going on around him.

The last act of the drama came when Noyes commissioned Smith to travel to Greencastle, Pennsylvania, as a missionary to a group of converts in that area. Smith agreed readily. It was probably not too difficult for him to persuade Mary to accompany him, and somehow—not specified—he managed to make George urge her to join the party. A week later George received a note from his wife announcing her return and asking that he meet her boat at Kingston. Only then did something in her manner suggest to him that all was not well, but his discipline held; he did not ask for any explanation.

Not until personal business called George himself to New York did he learn the facts. His friends, Mr. and Mrs. Lyvere, told him that not only had Abram tarried there with Mary for a week before continuing his journey but that they had broken their promise both to Noyes and to Cragin and spent the week in carnal union. After consulting together, it was decided that Mr. Lyvere should go to Putney to consult with John Noyes. Cragin supplied money for the trip and admonished Lyvere to report nothing but the truth. Thereupon he took the boat back to Rondout.

The scene of his meeting with his wife, after this revelation, is also difficult to credit. Mary met him smiling at the pier, but, as R. A. Parker has written, in *A Yankee Saint*, "the playful smile upon her face suddenly vanished. "'George,' she said, 'You know all. The secret is out and I thank God for revealing it. I will make a clean breast now, for I can carry on the works of darkness no longer.' She then related the simple facts without attempting to screen herself from judgment."

The fine old Victorian ring of these words is really too much for a modern ear. The denouement, in modern prose, sounds more convincing. Smith returned that night and insisted upon seeing Mary, who refused to see him. Next day the three spent in a long and violent three-sided quarrel. Smith swore that he had pleased God in all he had done and dared Cragin to sit in judgment. Mary merely confessed that she had believed Smith's arguments and had done wrong. George claimed that Smith was "under the delusions of the Devil."

By evening all were exhausted, Smith finally agreed to start once more for Putney and Cragin agreed that he would submit to Mr. Noyes's judgment. A quaint note was added here, when Smith suddenly became affectionate to George, of all people, and insisted on carrying a note from him to Noyes saying that he bore no unkind feelings to Smith, and, when George had rowed him across the river, insisted upon a farewell kiss of peace—from George.

This was very nearly the end of the story. The Cragins decided immediately to leave Rondout and, after selling most of their furniture, took the boat for New York. Fortunately for their peace of mind, a letter from John Humphrey Noyes reached them before they left. If it gave little comfort to the repentant Mary, it did at least reassure and approve of George. Noyes wrote: "Facts compel me to believe that Smith and Mrs. Cragin have violated the solemn engagement which they made me when I was in Kingston. I cannot avoid the conviction that it is my duty to withdraw myself from all fellowship with these persons. God has commanded believers to have 'no fellowship with the unfruitful works of darkness.' I see that no fellowship *can* exist between me and Smith. After all he has confessed and professed, after all that was said at K., after his unqualified covenant to do nothing in these matters without my knowledge and consent, he returns directly to works of evil concupiscence."

This was bad enough, but what outraged Noyes even more seriously was the fact that Smith, knowing himself to be an adulterer and deceiver, had gone into Pennsylvania under commission from his leader, as Noyes wrote, "at the very time when he had disqualified himself for that commission by a gross breach of faith toward me and the gospel which I preach. Without making known to me that breach of faith and so giving me an opportunity of clearing myself of responsibility, he has gone out as my representative and so has exposed me and the gospel to the reproach of his lewdness."

Noyes's advice to George Cragin was drastic.

Cut off that offending right hand and follow me. See that you are not entangled in the same net of Satan as Smith. Let no friendship paralyse your honesty and faithfulness to Christ. You are no longer bound by any obligation to keep the secrets or defend the character of Mrs. Cragin or Smith. Let them eat the fruit of their own doings. This seems cruel advice, but I protest, after deliberating the matter most calmly not in wrath or malice, but in all tenderness toward them as well as you, and in the fear of God, I can give no other in faith, conscience or friendship.

I could have stood by Smith in his war with the enemy at Kingston and in the storm of reproach which is coming upon him in the world, if he had done no more than was done before I was at Kingston. But now he has made his cause completely indefensible and I am compelled to abandon it. I advise you to get clear of all connection with it as quickly and quietly as possible. The treachery of this abandonment is not ours but his.

The *Monthly Record*, published at Putney for the Perfectionist family, notes that "Br. Noyes sent a copy of this letter to Br. Harrison at Meriden and by J.B.L. [Lyvere] to New York." On that same day, Smith arrived at Putney, having first thought to justify himself, but Br. Noyes refused to admit any justification, "showing him that he had been deluded by the wiles of the Devil and inflicted a grievous wound on the Church of Christ. Smith confessed his error and delusion and wrote letters acknowledging same, expressing abhorrence of what he had done and his approval of Br. Noyes's course in rejecting him."

These letters, which one would imagine difficult to write in the circumstances, flowed glib and unctuous, if ill-spelled, from his pen: "I feel a purpose of soul to hide myself in God, feeling a libberty to do so by His free consent and asshureance that he will carry me through safe." To another believer: "I hear testify that God does not condemn me and the reason why is because I am cleaving unto Him and do hate and turn away from this evil . . . but I do not say that I do not suffer by reason of my folly, for I do: but my sorrow as that which worketh repentance into life, which neadeth not to be repented of. I do expect to pass through soar conflicts and be dispirited and hated by many that loved me, but all this I am rezined to, having Jesus as my friend." He ends by asking his correspondent to show this letter "to all who will be benefitted by it."

We have no copy of the letter which the *Monthly Record* says reached Putney from George and Mary Cragin just before Smith left for home. It merely reports that Mrs. C. confessed her fault and strongly condemned it, asking no one to have confidence in her as a friend of the Gospel till she should prove by her deeds that she had returned to the right way. Guilty as she was, she wrote, she had been miserably deceived and deluded by Smith. (Here Smith objected to some of her statements but acknowledged that most were true in substance.) It appeared, the *Record* reported, "that S. and Mrs. C. entertained the belief that they were spiritually one, and that in the mind of the Lord she was his wife. He had taught her to believe that they were in an inner circle where the world had no right to know and judge of their actions."

Mary Cragin's letter to William Green, who had apparently been one of her close advisers during her New York period, is repentant but somewhat reproachful to her former mentor. "I suppose I must give you credit for a friendly interest in my behalf, though I must say I think you have a strange way of showing it. You censure me (very justly too) for leaning on an arm of flesh and yet you evidently want me to depend upon you for guidance. Why did you not give me such salutary counsel last winter, when I received your doctrines of Shakerism? My credulity led me to swallow Smith's assumptions that I was not, nor ever had been, Mr. Cragin's wife and that it was his province to break up such an ill-assorted marriage. This idea, once admitted, opened the door for licentiousness. Do not understand me as throwing off blame on others that belongs to myself. The past, my own nature with *all* its fruits I utterly condemn, *hate* and *forsake*. I know that Mr. Noyes, so far from being in any way responsible for such conduct, has from the first set his face as flint against it. If I had followed *his* instructions, instead of exalting you and Abram Smith into his place, I should not have had occasion to receive this terrible lesson."

The actual events of this period were first the removal of George Cragin and his family from New York to Uxbridge, Massachusetts, to the home of his sister and brother-in-law, who received them kindly. They asked no questions of their relatives about the past, but the brother-in-law offered to help George get a situation as bookkeeper, agent, or whatever berth in business he might prefer. His sister, in spite of being rigidly orthodox in her views, was still willing to introduce him as a preacher in her church. This

George gently refused and arranged to travel on to Putney, leaving Mary and their two children in Uxbridge.

In his *Story of a Life* Cragin confesses that the pitiable state of his wife, agonized with fear lest the powers in Putney would persuade George to cast her off and perhaps divorce her, tempted George to defer his journey to some indefinite future, but for a wonder, he resisted. "A well-contrived plot to throw me off the track. But far-seeing faith, that always connects the future with the present, was not to be cheated. That first instinct to go to Putney and report myself was a God-given one."

About the middle of September 1840 George set off. A nephew drove him to Worcester, where he could take the stage line to Vermont, a central terminus for many stage routes. He booked passage, taking great pleasure in riding on the box beside the driver, and reached Brattleboro late in the evening. Since Putney was still ten miles away, he stayed overnight and started on foot, before breakfast, arriving at Putney by ten o'clock that morning.

The meeting with John Noyes was sympathetic but quiet. As George wrote later:

> I thought that surely I would have a great deal to report about myself and others, the trials Mrs. Cragin and myself had passed through at Rondout, &c., but somehow or other I was all but speechless. I had very little to say about myself or anybody else. Egotism had left me. My thought did not seem to be my own but the thoughts of those around me. My trials were nothing. My sufferings too, what were they? I seemed to forget them. Thus, a week was spent in Putney but how short were the days composing it.
>
> The little circle of believers I found there appeared so different from any I had ever met before. All were so kind, so quiet, so thoughtful and studious and yet, in spirit, so free. If my sojourn in Rondout was a hell on earth, Providence had now compensated me with a heaven upon earth.

On his last day there, as he stood on the portico before taking his leave, Mr. Noyes, "who never talks unless he has something to say," asked him:

> "What are you going to do when you return to your family?"

"Find a situation in some counting-room or manufacturing establishment," George replied.

"I have a proposition to make to you," said Mr. N. "Return and spend the winter with me in studying the Bible and waiting on the will of God."

After a few moments I expressed some doubts as to the propriety of accepting an offer of so generous a magnitude, but Mr. Noyes forcibly replied that he used words not to conceal but to express his thoughts. It was enough. I stood corrected. I felt, as I had never felt before, that I had found a man of *solid* truth, who recognized no politeness, no human grace or embellishment, however fashionable, except it be of a pure, sincere, truth-loving heart. "Enough," I said. "I accept the offer as freely as you have extended it to me."

How Mary Cragin fared in her new surroundings may perhaps be deduced from a paper written by Harriet Noyes, the wife of John Humphrey. Harriet was utterly devoted to her husband's doctrines, even the most stringent, but she was also a woman of the greatest kindliness and forbearance and it must have been easier for Mary to confess to her than to the revered John Humphrey. What she wrote in 1840 would seem to us, more than a hundred years later, a pathetic story. Harriet wrote:

Mrs. C. told me that when she was a young lady she was called handsome, fascinating, by the opposite sex. She prided herself on having many admirers. She habitually enticed them with complaisance until she saw they were on the point of proposing marriage, and then treated them very coolly. After her marriage, when her attention was called to salvation from sin and she had commenced seeking it, the time arrived for her customary visit to Massachusetts to visit Mr. C's relatives. She was always greatly caressed and her vanity gratified by them, and her husband gave her many fine clothes for the occasion. This visit and salvation from sin were set before her to choose between: she concluded to defer seeking salvation until a more convenient season. Her husband went with her and, leaving her there, returned home. One of his relatives, a young gentleman, was professedly interested in Moral Reform and Abolition. He found no one among his friends equally interested in these subjects except Mrs. C. Consequently he had much conversation with her and an intimacy arose which led to great liberty. Mrs. C's husband came in good time. She resolved to confess the truth to him, and yet delayed it, walking under a great burden of sin until she confessed Christ a savior from sin. Then the load was taken from her for a time: however, it returned again and continued upon her until after she went to Kingston. She says the object of her visiting Mr. Smith's bed the first time was to converse on the subject, and consult him as to the expediency of confessing it to her husband: that he told her not to. She added that although Mr. S. made the first advances to their subsequent connection she considered she was as guilty as he in its continuation. She thought she was left to the commission of this gross wickedness as a reward for her concealment of her past transgression. She had thought many times that lust in her was destroyed but now she found it was hidden and restrained, and that John's rebuke had brought it to light. She wished me to tell him he was correct.

In a paper that she wrote, Mary Cragin was even harder on herself:

Indeed, every evil passion was very strong in me from my childhood, sexual desires, love of dress and *admiration, deceit, anger, pride*, but still I maintained a fair character before the world, and have been much flattered for amiability and other qualities which I did not possess. I was naturally very headstrong, determined to have my own way, was a very rebellious child, early got out from under the feeble control my parents exerted over me. I resolved never to obey a husband when his will opposed my own, unless disagreement would lead to an open quarrel that would be disgraceful in the eyes of the world. But enough of this heartsickening picture. My character may be summed up in a few words. I was like unto a whited sepulchre, fair to behold, but full of uncleanness. I eagerly embraced the doctrine of salvation from sin, feeling that it was just what I needed; for I could truly say of myself, "when I would do *good, evil* is present with me." In my ignorance, I supposed the work of regeneration would be instantaneously done when I exercised faith in Christ and confessed him a whole Savior. But I found, to my great astonishment, these former lusts returning. I was puzzled and distressed, and very much undervaluing the Bible as a book, prepared for another dispensation than this. I groped along in the dark, unconscious of the powers and deceitfulness of the Devil, and feeling that I was secure as to the final salvation, believing that what I saw wrong in me would wear out by some means or other. Now I begin to see that *Faith* all-important as it is, is the foundation stone on which to build virtue, temperance, knowledge, &c., and if we do not add these things to it, we have reason to fear that God will take away what we have.

I have never before been willing that everybody should know what a deceitful, vile woman I am by nature. Now I want them to know it *all*, because the salvation of Christ will be so much the more magnified in saving such a one as me.

The reactions of all three actors in this drama are difficult to credit in the light of today's thinking. John Noyes, one might have thought, considering Smith's recent behavior, would have suspected the sincerity of his promises as early as the visit to

Mary Cragin and George Cragin were converted to Perfectionism by John Humphrey Noyes in 1840.

Rondout in May. He might also have been penetrating enough to recognize that Mary was persuadable to almost any extent and that her husband was not only enslaved by her but a total convert to Perfectionist doctrine. Abram Smith was apparently even more persuasive than his leader, since as late as that spring, Noyes wrote to a friend that Smith was "faithful and true and growing like the calves of the stall." We need to know the explanation of these conflicting facts.

But even more importantly, we need to know what kind of woman was Mary Cragin. Dutiful daughter, devout church member, passionately responsive wife, easy convert to one and then another religious creed, fanatic believer in every new doctrine that came along, too easily persuadable, credulous, naive, trustful, unquestioning of those in whom she had placed her faith? A childlike innocent led astray by a sophisticated man—or a coquette, a devious and subtle woman seeking her own pleasure?

Thirty years after her death, her husband wrote that she was not an intellectual. Others differed. A contemporary Community member wrote in the *Circular*, January 11, 1852, a year after her death: "We miss the energy of her intellect. She had a wisdom and good sense so ready that it seemed pure instinct, but she had also a powerful intellect. I never was with her without admiring the relish she had for knowledge and her perseverance in learning. She gave new impetus to the spirit of education."

Another commentator wrote: "She was remarkable for her appreciation of life and fondness for all that was lively and sparkling. Vivacity was the peculiar element of her character. She was fond of natural scenery, music, wit, poetry, children—whatever was bright and effervescent. She loved to taste everything in its freshness." Robert Allerton Parker wrote in *A Yankee Saint:* "There could be no half-measures with Mary. Present tense, Imperative Mood. Such was her secret of living."

If her husband had decried her intellect, the Community thought otherwise and decided to appoint her as co-editor with George of the *Circular*, the new paper they were about to issue. But it was not to be. One week later—July 15—the printing press at Oneida burned to the ground. Friends of Mary wrote later that to edit a religious paper in New York City had been her dream for years, but that seems uncharacteristic of the Mary of Rondout days. The writer added however that "her great beauty was in *being;* her life was more effective than her pen—she *acted* history and truth more than she wrote it." Whether or not this was true, we shall never know.

We do know that she had once been, by choice, a teacher. Early in her last spring, she was sent to Wallingford to start a school in the new community. She was enthusiastic about the project, writing to Harriet Noyes, "I see the absolute necessity of attending to the mental as well as the spiritual cultivation," which chimes with the later comment that "she had a powerful intellect and a relish for knowledge." This talent was recognized in the Community, since one article notes that in the children's department "her loss seems most irreparable. She combined the faculty of government with that of pleasing. She could become a child to children and not lose their respect, correct them without provoking them to wrath."

No one mentions her appearance, and the only picture of her that we have is a very bad, chromo-like portrait which shows her as plain, to put it kindly, with a serious, almost melancholy expression, but here again, apparently is a contradiction. What she must have had was a personality so attractive that mere beauty was far outdistanced. "As a social genius we can scarcely expect to see her like again. Her ear for heart music was exquisitely susceptible, her talent was for promoting unity by the magnetism of her spirit and the example of her manners." Or, as Harriet Skinner wrote, "her genius was so universal we can hardly tell where she is missed most. Every department of the community seems bereft, like children without a mother."

Only ten years after John Humphrey Noyes had enjoined George Cragin to break all connection with Mary, "to clear himself of the wreck if he had to jump into the ocean," we find him and other Community members calling her "the foremost woman of the little band which in 1848 formed the Oneida Association." The shocking accident in 1851 in which she drowned left not only Noyes but the rest of the Community shaken and grieving. Pages of the *Circular* were devoted to accounts of the tragedy. Letters and panegyrics were published for months to come, praising what Noyes had once called "that offending right hand" and now called "our sweetest and best fellow-laborer."

Resolve these contradictions and perhaps we shall have the key not only to her own nature but to her strange life story and the secret of one episode in the pre-history of the Community. Mary Cragin was drowned with Eliza Allen in the sloop *Rebecca*

Ford which Abram Smith had given to the Community the year before. The vessel capsized in a squall of wind on the Hudson River almost exactly opposite the village of Rondout, on July 25, 1851.

The actual order of events after the departure of the Cragins from Rondout is not wholly clear. From New York the Cragins travelled to Uxbridge, Massachusetts, to the home of George's sister, where he deposited Mary and the children while he made his pilgrimage to Putney and John Noyes. What he probably expected was a total divorcement from the Putney branch and a severe criticism from John Noyes. Instead, he was met with sympathy and an invitation to come, with his whole family and join the Putney group. George felt, as he wrote later, that he had met a man of solid truth. The invitation was accepted with joy.

What with the increasing hostility and turbulence in Putney, the establishment of other branch communes came into being. The spacious farm of the Henry Allen's at Wallingford, Connecticut, was made a member branch of the greatest use and the longest life, beginning in 1851. Smaller groups were formed in northern Vermont, in Newark, New Jersey, in Manlius, New York—not all successful nor long-lived, but evidence of the spreading belief of Perfectionism. Mary Cragin's heart-felt repentence led her into a life of utter devotion to the Community, or as John Noyes said, made her "our sweetest and best fellow laborer." George, her husband, was for twenty years one of the stalwart Central Members, a devoted laborer in the Community vineyard.

BUILDING THE ONEIDA COMMUNITY

THE LEAD EDITORIAL in the *Spiritual Magazine* for December 1, 1849, is entitled *Our Work* and was probably written by John Humphrey Noyes: "There is one business which we acknowledge ourselves bound to accomplish in this world, and we say only one. That is 'to bear witness to the *truth.*'"

How this object was primarily to be accomplished presented no problem to John Noyes. From the days of his long struggle following his astounding announcement of sinlessness in New Haven, he conceived what was to be a life-long passion for publishing. Through the rise and fall of nine periodicals, the publication of a half-dozen pamphlets and several books, he never gave up his belief that by this means could best be achieved the "one business" he was bound to accomplish. Of all the enterprises which the Community undertook, religious or secular, the instrument of the Press was the means by which he hoped to revolutionize the souls of men. He planned to continue publishing at Oneida immediately.

But as it happened, the recommencement of their printing was destined to wait for another year. A prior necessity supervened—adequate accommodations must come first; the new house must be built; not quite the "Chateau" which Mr. Noyes had promised his wife, but the first Mansion House, built for themselves, by themselves. "All hands," they wrote, "whenever free from other necessary occupations, were merrily busy on the house. Even the women joined the sport. The house was ready for occupation, although not finished, before winter."

In this fledgling colony were only thirteen men, and of this number were one shoemaker, one lead-pipe maker, one millwright, one architect, one merchant, two sawyers, one blacksmith, one printer, one cabinet-maker, one stonemason, one teamster—and John Noyes.

Providence, always on hand when needed, had actually provided the indispensable. A new joiner, Erastus Hamilton, was an enterprising young architect from nearby Syracuse, who with John Humphrey Noyes, "one moon light night, with the North Star as a guide point" (*Old Mansion House Memories*, by Harriet M. Worden), staked out the ground for the foundation walls of the new house. In the nick of time, again, when the little group of amateurs who had never built a stone wall in their lives were faced with this formidable job, a Mr. Ruggles from Baldwinsville appeared. Naturally, given John Humphrey Noyes's proverbial "luck," this gentleman was an experienced stonemason. Parker writes: "Under the direction of Mr. Ruggles, the job of stonework on the cellar walls was undertaken enthusiastically. As chief assistants, Mr. Ruggles had Daniel P. Nash (one of the original members of Jonathan Burt's little commune) and Noyes, himself. Soon they became expert masons." And obviously, with the Burt sawmill and plenty of timber on their new domain, they lacked for nothing—except money.

Why did all the Owenite and Fourierist Associations fail? Noyes, had an opinion of this, "The fondness for land had much to do with their failures. Farming is about the hardest and longest of all roads to fortune; and it is the kind of labor in which there is the most uncertainty as to modes and theories, and of course the largest chance for disputes and discords in such complex bodies as Associations. We should have advised the Phalanxes to limit their land investment to a minimum and put their strength into some form of manufacture. Almost any kind of factory would be better than a farm for a Community nursery." Noyes may have been right but the rival communes did not take his advice.

On June 12, 1850, the Oneida Community's periodical *The Free Church Circular* recorded that two young men, Fourierists from Baltimore, called on them "for the purpose of inspection and inquiry." They asked first what system of accounts Oneida used in the labor department; what regulations for stimulating labor and making sure of its just reward. "They seemed," the editor wrote, "considerably astonished to learn that there was no system of accounts, no formal regulations; that everyone was free to labor as much or as little as he chose and there was no cash settlement in a written scale of rewards."

Fourier's original specifications for associational living were not only grandiose—he foresaw proliferation of his communes over the whole civilized world—but extremely elaborate, with divisions into groups and series, a total world brotherhood, a common language, a uniform life style. Some of his ideas were delightfully fantastic. Because children liked to play in the mud, they were to be organized into scavenging groups known as Little Hordes who would dispose of "dirt and refuse"—a garbage brigade, in other words. The stars and planets were sentient beings like ourselves who fell in love and reproduced their kind, aged, decayed, and died. Men would ultimately grow tails equipped with eyes. The sea, losing its saltiness, would turn into lemonade. The climate would be everywhere the same and wild beasts would be replaced by "anti-lions," "anti-sharks," "anti-rats," and so on. Constantinople would be the capital of the world, ruled by the Omniarch. Poor Fourier, after a life of gorgeous dreams and impoverished and sordid reality, died on his knees in 1837.

But his ideas—or the less fantastic of them—were espoused first in this country by Albert Brisbane and after him by a number of other prestigious persons: Horace Greeley, Ripley, Dana, Channing, Lowell, and others, and the most sensible, if not the most successful commune was Brook Farm, in 1844. The largest and longest-lived was the North American Phalanx at Red Bank, New Jersey. Of the other Fourierist Associations or Phalanxes, according to the *History of American Socialisms*, fourteen apparently did not live long enough to have a history. Of those reported in the Macdonald MS, "Twelve lasted less than a year; two, one year each; four, between one and two years; three, two years; four, between two and three years; one, between three and four years; one, four years; one, five years; one, six years; one, twelve years; one (it is said), seventeen years. All died young, and most of them before they were two years old."

The Oneida Community's original statement that "horticulture is our principle means of subsistence" held true only until some more profitable means was discovered to take its place, and attested by its almost unanimous adoption of any kind of industrial enterprise which would make it a living. John Humphrey Noyes has been accused of being too changeable, but this may have been one of the lifesaving characteristics that kept the Community afloat for so many years. He was ready to admit a mistake, erase it, and try something else. In one of their evening meetings he spoke of the cultivation of a flexible will in small matters. "Pliancy of will seems to be especially pleasing to Christ; it gives the social atmosphere a more than downy softness" (*Circular*, January 20, 1859). In large matters he was immovable; in small, he was willing, as they used to say, to "out and try."

One lifesaving attribute of his followers, whether inculcated by their leader or inherited from generations of laborious Yankees, was a unanimous willingness to work hard to accomplish their goal. And lest today's modern young communitarians, who, in some cases at least, seem to live in terror of being "structured" (i.e., organized, asked, expected, or, worst of all, *told* to take part in any group effort), assume that their predecessors at Oneida suffered a kind of industrial slavery, it should be understood that there no one was obliged to work. In the Oneida Community, working under a sense of duty or, as they used to say, "legally," was strongly criticized whenever it occurred, which was not often. Work, they believed, must be freely chosen, "under inspiration." Visitors inquired what they did about the lazy ones. The answer was simple: they seldom had any lazy ones.

They turned their hands to any work that would bring in an honest penny. There was a sawmill on the property which meant a good water power. Naturally they sawed wood from their wood lots and later, in their grist mill, made and sold flour. They planted broom corn and made and sold brooms.

By the *Second Annual Report* they counted 172 members and the next year, 205. More hands to work, but also, more mouths to feed. By 1850 they had erected "a large and very substantial building for mechanical purposes on the ground formerly occupied by the old Indian saw mill." They had a new circular saw, with which they made lath and pickets, and a new shingle machine; they had a flouring mill, a machine shop, and a shop for wagon-makers and carpenters, with appropriate machinery. They planted an orchard of young fruit trees, plus a large number of bearing fruit trees already on the domain, and their head horticulturist, Mr. Thacker, was in charge of a nursery containing 2,300 trees of different kinds. They grew and sold nursery stock, vines, strawberry plants, whatever found a market.

Some of their efforts died a-borning, or, at least, lived a

very short time. They thought of making baskets out of osier willow and invested $25.00 in the experiment, but found it uneconomical. Their maritime ambitions faded in 1851 with the sinking of their sloop that carried Mary Cragin to her death. Sewall Newhouse had been a trapper in his youth and urged the Community to send out parties to trap or at least to buy furs from trappers in the Adirondacks, but it never came to much. Men, women, and even children learned to braid palm-leaf hats. Someone suggested making embroidered slippers for gentlemen, but although some of the young girls took it up eagerly, their enthusiasm soon faded. At one time—this was later, in the 1860s—they made and sold some plows and farm wagons, but nothing important came of that, either, although they did make and sell wheel-spokes and scuffle hoes.

In 1852, a new member, Mr. Ellis, "introduced to the Community the art of making rustic seats, tables, etc., for garden use and ornament." No relic of this "art," that I know of, has survived, but judging from old photographs, this is no great loss. As the *Circular* described it, "rough cedar sticks were fashioned into various fantastic forms of furniture." Perhaps, considering their own recent enthusiasm for Victoriana, modern critics should not be too disparaging of this craft. However that may be, the communists "readily disposed of all they made at good prices"—which, Heaven knows, they needed—"and exhibited one of their seats at the State Fair where it won a diploma" and two years later at a Fair in Utica "attracted much attention and gained a silver medal." The *Circular* added: "Our friends will appreciate these little indications of success as favors from God: the more pleasant, as happening in a place where we have been somewhat misunderstood and abused." This, of course, is a reference to their ordeal in the Utica County Courts.

Beginning in the new little commune at Wallingford, Connecticut, in 1851, they began to make bags, carpet bags and a patent lunch bag, designed by Mr. Noyes. Later, as the bag business grew in volume, it was moved to Oneida where both men and women worked, often in "Bees," stitching the bags. This business had continued with fair success until 1866 when it was felt that competition with city manufacturers was too sharp and, probably more important, that their other major industries were absorbing all their labor and attention.

A natural development from their original interest in horticulture was the selling of their product, first by peddler's carts which traveled throughout the area and later, in the form of preserved fruits and vegetables, at first as an experiment, with tomatoes put up in bottles. A note in the *Circular* in 1856 announced "Our preserved tomatoes in cans and jars have been tested in the neighboring cities, and are liked. Preparations are being made for enlarging this business the coming season. Mr. Pitt is now on a tour of inquiry and inspection with a view to gathering the best information in all that relates to raising and preserving fruit. Preparations for building a fruit house are in progress." This experience met with a gratifying success and presently the Community expanded the business to include corn and asparagus and a number of fruits in the form of sauce and jellies and jams preserved in tin cans and glass jars.

As early as 1854, John Humphrey Noyes, facing their worst financial crisis, recalled that two of their members had originally been what were called, "peddlers," and he suggested that a peddling department be organized to sell Community products. Parker writes in *A Yankee Saint* that "inspired by the enthusiasm of their leader, all were soon begging, men and women alike, for the privilege of going out. One man cried that he would shoulder a razor-grinder 'and joyfully, too,' if it would serve the Community. So the Community peddlers ventured forth, two by two, on foot like the disciples of Christ. Usually they were not absent for more than a week. On their return these men were cleansed by a thorough scrubbing in the turkish bath and the criticism of their comrades. They carried pins and needles, silk thread, combs, lace edging, ink, collars, palm-leaf hats, and other products manufactured at one time or another by the Community. They acquired a thorough training in the Yankee art of salesmanship and soon they no longer trudged the dusty roads on foot, but rode in 'the cars!'"

Work in the Community was, let us admit, carefully "structured." The *Circular*, April 19, 1855, reported:

> The partial organization for the spring and summer business was reported today. Two men are nominated to lead the work of the general domain, four men to direct the garden and furnish work to all applicants, three to have charge of the teams, etc., etc. ... The trap and bag manufacturing will probably for the most part be suspended during the summer. The above organization leaves, as

was intended, a large portion of the Community men, women and children free and moveable, so that they can be called into any department where help is needed and can shift and alternate employment easily.

The trap business began as so often happens, with one person and that person, as we say a "character." Sewall Newhouse, like John Humphrey Noyes, was born in Brattleboro, Vermont. His family migrated to what was then called "the western country," Oneida County, New York, where Sewall became a hunter and trapper of extraordinary skill. He began to make an improved type of animal trap. He worked laboriously, with a few crude implements, in his blacksmith shop in the tiny settlement of Oneida Castle where local hunters, especially Indians, brought him a brisk trade. Before he left his forge to join the Oneida Community in 1849, he was making and selling two thousand traps a year.

As Parker writes, "Every year he explored and reexplored the wild country around Oneida Lake. His cronies never tired of repeating the stories of his feats of running and wrestling. His almost fabulous strength was never misused or brutalized. On the contrary, Newhouse was gentle and shy. A strange character, individual to the point of eccentricity, and the last man in the world one would have thought could be induced to join in the Community at the Indian saw mill. However, as early as 1835 he had been attracted to the advanced views of the New York Perfectionists. Almost fifteen years later he and his family became members of the Oneida Community."

To quote the *Circular*, June 27, 1864: "For several years after this but little attention was paid to the trap business. A few dozen traps were made occasionally by Mr. Newhouse in the old way but it was not until 1855, under a call for traps from Chicago and New York, that practical interest was first directed to this branch of manufacture with a view to its extension."

What happened next is an amusing story. John Humphrey Noyes, who, oddly enough, always had an attraction to things mechanical, grew curious about Newhouse's secret method of making traps and wished to join him in the work. At first the crusty old trapper practically held the door against his leader. Apparently it took all of Noyes's persuasiveness to be allowed to enter the little trap shop and to learn the secrets of the craft. After a bit he persuaded Newhouse to let one or two of the young men join them and during this teaching process the two older men became fast friends.

The next year the trap shop, which had been employing only three hands, was moved to a larger room and connected with a water power. Several other young men were inducted into the craft and in a short time the enlarged group devised mechanical appliances to take the place of hand labor. Where previously the steel spring had been processed wholly by hand—two men with a heavy two-hand sledge and a heavy hammer delivering one hundred and twenty blows—it was finally bent, bowed, and tempered by machinery. At a later date the Community began making trap chains, also mainly by machine power.

A meticulous business history of the Oneida Community, after describing these early efforts, would be obliged to admit that they were often unprofessional, amateurish, and homemade. The communists themselves recorded that in the first nine years—1848 through 1857—they "sank $40,000 in our own education, which is like sinking an oil well—expensive at first but lucrative afterwards, *if you 'strike oil.'*" Fortunately, they did strike oil, but it took a lot of learning first.

SELF-IMPROVEMENT

IN A PERIOD when Sabbatarianism was not only prevalent but in many cases rigidly observed, the Oneida Community's heterodox attitude on the subject occasioned much disapproval. From the beginning, the Oneida Associationists did not observe Sunday in the orthodox way. Most people, they said, especially those who went to church, washed and dressed up in their Sunday best "so as to make a showing of the outer man." This was not The Community's way. The Sunday Spirit of common society outside was sleepy and listless, averse to serious thought. The Communists called it the Sunday Stupor and criticized it severely. "Slicking up" on Sunday at Oneida was a different thing; they "dressed up" their grounds, not their persons; they called a Bee every Sunday morning for an hour or so to "dress up" their door-yard and out-of-the-way places and felt there was no blasphemy in this since "work was worship"; their grounds were their meeting-house, consecrated to the Lord and therefore as sacred as any place could be.

Although special emphasis was naturally placed upon the education and training of the children, their elders did not escape criticism. Ascending fellowship, a doctrine upon which John Humphrey Noyes placed much emphasis—companionship so that the drawing of the fellowship was upward—applied as much to the old as the young. In an Evening Meeting in 1856 they had considerable to say concerning the evils of horizontal fellowship among the young, its tendency to produce levity and superficiality, but they thought it only fair to recognize the equal danger of "packing together the old." This tended to produce an opposite evil which was just as bad—discontent, irritability and fault-finding. The old and infirm were apt to be querulous and cross. In some ways the young were actually their superiors—in cheerfulness, good-nature and a hopeful view of life. For the old to give themselves up to horizontal fellowship and stimulate one another's bad tendencies by talk, and especially to criticize the young, was self-destructive. The old need the society of the young and should seek their fellowship. There had been some temptation from the cross spirit which, they said, was a cursed, devilish thing and should be crushed as a serpent.

In a Community where improvement was the chief aim, young and old were exhorted to exercise their faculties, to learn the truth about everything and thereby enlarge their sphere of liberty. This, they said, applied equally to all ages; the young were apt to allow momentary pleasure to seize their attention; the old were often too much occupied by labor and employment. The two should meet in the spirit of improvement which would make labor sport and sport, labor; in other words, the amalgamation of employments—the work of the old with the play of the young.

The commonest labor, like washing, was dispatched with a buoyancy of spirit that was contagious. Much enthusiasm in labor was often created by Bees in which the whole force of the Community, men, women and children, was turned on to some special job like harvesting a field of corn. At such times the whole Community would be marshaled under a spreading butternut tree near the house by the stirring music of fife and drum, produced by men whose grandfathers were at Lexington and Bunker Hill. The children, a merry and excited group, brought up the rear with their guardians. In a surprisingly short time the field would be cleared and the march back to the house with the fife and drum at the head of the column would be made amid great enthusiasm.

Another kind of game is described:

> This susceptibility to sweeping enthusiasms which left a deep educational mark on every member was a peculiar, I might almost say wonderful feature of society in the Oneida Community, and it was constantly taking place. I remember when I was a boy someone began to play chess one evening in the parlor after the Evening Meeting. Interest in the game immediately seemed to spread and became intense. Chess boards multiplied, and for months silent but tense groups could be seen everywhere, either playing chess or

earnestly watching the moves of the contestants. Before the wave had subsided nearly everyone in the Community could play chess intelligently and several were experts. A similar wave of enthusiasm for the study of phonography supplied the Community with a score of expert home stenographers whose success in reporting Mr. Noyes's "Home Talks" and in preserving the immense archives of the Community has been invaluable.

An article, unsigned but evidently written by a life-long member of the Community, is entitled *What Held the O.C. Together:*

The world at large has always looked upon the experiences of the Oneida Community as little less than miraculous in respect to its unity and power of agreement. *The most important influence in producing these good results, and in holding the society together was undoubtedly its unity of religious belief and its resolute purpose to subdue selfishness.* A man's conduct is controlled by the secret motives of his heart. If the motives are unselfish, the conduct will be unselfish and harmonious.

The result of these beliefs, of the sincerity of which there can be no question, was that the members of the community regarded themselves as a peculiar people, chosen of God to do a certain work. All selfishness, therefore, must be put away and every heart be made pure.

It was a school for the discipline and refinement of character, and it was deemed important to shield it as much as possible from worldly influences. Contact with the outside world, even through one's natural relations, was to be avoided; and as in the early years when the Community depended on agriculture as the leading means of subsistence, about the only necessary contact was through the man who drove our team to Oneida every day to mail letters, get the New York *Tribune*, and make a few purchases. He was the financial agent, handling all filthy lucre and occupying an exposed position.

This early period, when we were so secluded and free from outside influences, when we had no hired help whatever, but the members did all their own work, including even the most menial service, when our food and clothing were of the plainest and scantiest, was the time of greatest faith in God's care over us, and in Mr. Noyes's inspiration and in the final triumph of our system. Many providences which occurred from time to time strengthened this faith and bound the Community together.

Secluded they certainly were, but in spite of their "school for the refinement of character," the old Adam—or, in this case, the old Eve—broke loose occasionally. It was all very harmless. A charming bit of reminiscence dictated by an ex-member, Mrs. Minerva Norton, when she was past ninety years old, tells of escapades in her childhood.

Minerva was evidently not the ring-leader in this mischief, but her leader was Harriet Worden, who, all her life, was criticized for what they called, "the Cook Spirit." This regrettable spirit was supposed to have been inherited from her mother's family, the Cooks, who had migrated to Manlius from Stone Arabia, New York, where her grandfather had been a Revolutionary War hero. This was not disapproved of by the Community, many of whose forebears had served in that war, but because certain uncles and cousins of Cook blood were known to be "worldly" and had been unregenerate financial successes. Harriet, who was my paternal grandmother, died before I was born, and I have always regretted that I could not have known her. She sounds like a delightfully naughty little girl. The tale of her childish adventures, as Minerva tells it, is amusing:

> I remember well being associated with Harriet and I will tell you one or two memories. One day (about this time of year) there was to be a corn-cutting bee in a field west, now a part of the golf

Minerva Norton joined Harriet Worden on various childhood escapades.

links. Harriet said to me, "We don't want to cut corn. Let's go exactly away from it, in the opposite direction." So we started up *East* hill and walked and walked until we came to Indian Town. There we met a big Indian. He did not pay any attention to us, but we were frightened.

Then we passed a house where two white girls, younger than we, were swinging on a gate, and they called to us and asked us to come to play with them. "There is no one at home," they said. So we went into the house. But in the house, in a bed in the kitchen, was a sick woman and another woman also. She (the other woman) was baking apples. The sick woman wanted us to sing for her. We stayed in the kitchen quite a while and sang to her. I don't know what we sang. Harriet and I could always sing duets. The woman, I think, had consumption. She was the wife of Bill Hamilton. She liked our songs.

After a time, two other girls came and with these girls and the two first, we went to the barn where there was a girl's playhouse in one corner. And there we played with dolls and played all sorts of games, staying all the afternoon until night time. When asked our names, we gave fictitious names—Harriet was "Harriet Cragin" and I was "Minerva Allen." At home we had not been missed so we did not get a criticism. Harriet was always leader, but I was a *good* follower.

Many times we went off like this to satisfy the need for adventure in Harriet. She liked to reach out beyond her everyday life, and she had a social need, a liking for meeting and manipulating people: a family trait I think, for I saw it in Cornelia, too, and in a measure in Joanna, and in Pierrepont in a bigger way.

Many times we went off walking like the above, and coming to a house, would ask for a drink of water and often we were invited into the house. At one place, I remember, beyond the mill, there lived a family named Rossun or some such name (I do not know its spelling exactly). There lived a very pretty girl who had a melodian. When she invited us in there we had a chance to see the melodian, something we had so much wished to see.

One winter Harriet and I did some fancy dancing at an entertainment for the family. We dressed in ballet costume, with red morocco shoes made for us by Mr. Van Velzer.

One of Harriet's adventures with Alice Ackley carried them, by borrowing a horse and buggy from the barn, as far as Quality Hill, and they were missed when it grew late. And finally when they returned, I happened along as Mr. Hamilton was giving Harriet a severe criticism, telling her she had a bad spirit. I remember her reply was, "I will examine myself and see."

Harriet M. Worden came to the Oneida Community as a little girl of nine and later edited the *Circular*.

What he said to Alice is not recorded. She, my other grand-mother, was quieter and perhaps more tractable than Harriet but she had an independent spirit, too. I remember that even in old age after a lifetime of strict temperance, when the Prohibition Law

Alice Ackley Kinsley was brought to the Oneida Community as a baby and later became a gifted musician.

was passed, she refused to be dictated to and asked her son to bring her a bottle of whiskey which I'm sure she never drank. It was purely a gesture of defiance.

The "good men and women" whom George Miller remembered with deep admiration lived in what they were taught to call a "school, for the education of their hearts as well as their minds." Criticism was one of the most important classes they attended. The lessons were vividly expounded. The *Free Church Circular* reported on December 20, 1850:

> That state of exquisite attention to other spirits which will subdue attention to our own individuality is the only condition in which we can become social beings. M——[her name is not given in the paper] was "remarkable for originality and activity of mind and will. This was good for her in the world," the critic said, "as a chestnut-burr is good for the nut in squirrel time. While we are in the world where we are likely to be eaten by squirrels, God has put a burr over us. It is good for that time—for the burr cannot be eaten; but when the time comes, the burr must be taken off. We cannot be social beings with a chestnut burr over us."

Little scraps from journals or diaries are always revealing. Faint handwriting—this by my great-grandmother Julia Ackley—tells mostly of goings and comings but occasional comment gives the flavor of the time. "Mr. Carr returned from Albany this afternoon and reported good success, sold 8 dozen traps." And then, "Mr. Lawton criticized—how he does have to be come down upon! It's surprising. My name came in the first group and I earnestly pray for an ambition to do the best I can." But she does not tell what her criticism was. "I arose this morning as well as usual but about 8 o'clock was taken with cold chills. Very soon a fever came on, pain in my back and head. I do not know what to attribute it to unless it is sympathy with Mr. Ackley, as he had been troubled the same way. I confess my separation from my false spirit either in him or any one else, and confess my union with Christ and the Primitive Church."

Poor sweet *good* little Julia. So darling and uncomplaining about being separated from her husband whom she adored and, since this was a "special love" and "the marriage spirit," she not only criticized herself but was criticized by the Committee who periodically examined OC members. She was a tiny little creature, her dark hair brushed demurely behind her ears, and she had a lovely smile. I don't remember her, of course, but I love her just the same.

Merely from looking at her sweet, sad little face in her photographs, I cannot imagine her struggling with recalcitrant children. She had been sent to deal with her only surviving son, an unmanageable teenager, and Julia worried about him. "Mrs. Newhouse writes that Albert is in a hard, disobedient state, has had a good deal of criticism but it does not seem to effect a cure. O my Father, I pray that my heart may be softened so that thou canst hear a mother's prayer for him, that his heart may be touched by the Spirit of Christ. I pray that he may have a new conversion." I know very little about Albert, except that he left the Community —just when, I don't know, but he died twenty years after this touching little prayer, in 1874.

Alice, Julia's daughter, was only seven years old when this diary was kept, but even at that age she worried her mother. "It has been a busy day, spiritually as well as otherwise. I have been stirred up about Alice"—my own gentle and beloved grandmother who cannot be imagined as anything else—"She has had a boistrous, disobedient spirit upon her for several days. I pray for wisdom in dealing with her."

Nearly twenty-five years later, Julia's diary, still faithfully kept, had a grimmer tone. Affairs in the Community were, as they said "in a chowder." Members were leaving, there were quarrels between the Central members. The possible sale of Wallingford Community was discussed. In May Mr. Noyes proclaimed his son, Theodore, his successor as leader of the Community, and in June Myron Kinsley, who had apparently deserted the Community, returned. It was hoped that peace would return too, but Julia's entry for January 1878 carried bad news again. "A great explosion took place between Mr. Noyes and Theodore, the latter getting very angry. The battle rages." And in February, she noted briefly, "Another violent eruption about the Community." That summer the blow fell—"Sunday the 22nd, night, Mr. Noyes and Myron left for parts unknown." The next day, "Mr. Pitt left for somewhere" and "Myron came back from somewhere."

At the end of August, at the suggestion of Mr. Noyes—still absent—the Community voted to abandon their social theory, after which a number of the couples married "after the fashion of the world." Julia Ackley had little to say except, "I confess a quiet spirit amidst great tumult. A great revolution is going on. I pray for grace to behave well through it all." And at the end, "We have all signed for our stock this 10th day of November, 1880. The day of voting has come and the directors chosen. Thank the Lord it is all over with." And on January 1, 1881, "We are all joint stock today but I don't see but I can be just as thankful as I ever was and our first evening meeting in the East Room was rather crowded."

Two little notes at the end have a slightly saturnine tinge. "A good many have gone to work today that haven't done but precious little for months and months," and "bought the first spool of thread today that I have bought in the Community 33 years."

Of all the children in the Children's House in those early days, I would give large odds that there was not one sweeter or more amenable than "Little Jessie Baker." Gentle, unassuming, Community-born, and Community raised, she accepted without a murmur the pattern of that strange Association, framed on the Bible pattern and called Bible Communism, which taught the children that their parents were the *entire Community* and, as she wrote later, to make ingrained in the older people the feeling that they were mothers and fathers, grandmothers, aunts and uncles of *all* of children. Nevertheless, it was found comfortable and a pleasant thing for a child to have a special "Community father" where any, by death or inadvertence, had missed a *natural* father.

Aunt Jessie wrote:

My mother chose no Community father for me. I was seven years old when Eleazer Hatch suddenly became convinced that I was his daughter. He was under conviction of sin and in condemnation of spirit and said he knew such experience would be just his luck. Mother felt somewhat concerned about this late claiming of me, but I was delighted to have a father. So then my name was no longer Jessie Baker but Jessie Hatch and, to my great relief, I was rid of the suggestive rhyme—

Little Jessie Baker
Take her up and shake her.

THE BRANCH COMMUNES

I N 1851 a new branch of the Oneida Community was begun on a farm legally inherited by them under a will drawn up by Henry Allen and his wife. A letter from George Cragin to the editors of the *Free Church Circular*, published in the issue of March 13, 1851, describes this unusual gift:

An Assignment.

To the brethren and Sisters in Christ Jesus:

Know all by these presents, that we, Henry Allen and Emily H., his wife, both of Wallingford, New Haven County, State of Connecticut, being of sound and disposing mind, do make and ordain this, our last will and testament, in words following, viz:—We will that all our debts be paid, by our executor hereinafter named; and the remainder of our estate, both real and personal, together with *ourselves*, we do give unto Jesus Christ and his church, to have and to hold the same forever. And we do hereby appoint Mr. John H. Noyes as our executor, to see that distribution is made to everyone as they have need.

Given under our hand and seal of the *Cross*, this 13th day of February, 1851.

Henry Allen

Emily H. Allen

"I heartily approve of the consecration that brother Henry

and sister Emily have made above, and hesitate not to join with them in making the same consecration of myself and all I possess.

Eliza A. Allen."

"Mr. and Mrs. Allen visited the Brooklyn commune in the winter of 1851 and became earnest and whole-hearted partners of the Association. They carried home the spirit of self-improvement, and soon afterwards sent an invitation to Mrs. Cragin to come and help them organize a family school and put them on the track of education. She was very happy to be a missionary to the region of the birthplace of Perfectionism and, in the spring, while Mr. Noyes was absent in England, she went to Connecticut and spent four or five weeks. This was the beginning of the Wallingford Association," as noted in the *Circular*, December 28, 1851.

The property was near the village of Wallingford, Connecticut, at the foot of Mount Tom and beside the Quinnipiac River. The farm buildings, plain and without even such "modern conveniences" as Oneida could boast, became a much-loved and valued station for rest and change for the Oneida members and was the only branch to remain in their possession to the very end of the Oneida Community.

Twenty-five years later, in the *American Socialist*, March 30, 1876, Harriet Skinner described it with great affection: "The faith and principles, the tastes and sentiments of the two families are one. Their property is one. They have many customs in common. The Evening Meeting, handed down from the original Putney Community to the Oneida Community, is as dear to the Wallingford Community as to either of its progenitors. Sunday is not observed at either commune, but a meeting every evening is as constant as the stars. A leader is chosen to give direction to the discussions and exercises.

"The domestic arrangements of the two Communes are very much alike. Private rooms for individuals and common sitting-rooms for all. Two meals a day—breakfast at 8, dinner at 3. Fare much the same. Wallingford, living nearer the seashore, has shellfish oftener and fresher than they do at O.C., but unbolted wheat, milk and fruit constitute the staples here and there."

"The family at O.C. is four times as large as this family and all arrangements are in proportion. W.C. is comparatively rustic; small wooden buildings without ornament inside or out. Our

hall is a plain, unshapely room, and for music we only have a parlor organ and some singing girls. Our books could be put into one
alcove of the O.C. library. It is always easy to get up a 'Bee' for
any emergency, for any extra job, and carry it by storm."

"Horticulture, the leading means of subsistence," was the
motto at Oneida Community at the time the Wallingford commune was started. This, and the fact that the property had previously been a farm, made it natural that market gardening was the
first industry of the WC family. As Harriet Skinner wrote, "it was
just the one to develop and educate the Bee spirit. Bees were sometimes called before breakfast or after an early supper, when whatever produce had been picked was fresh for delivery in the morning. Meriden, six miles away, was an eager market for peas and pie-
plant, radishes and cabbages, spinach and asparagus or whatever
crop the ground could yield. Strawberries," Harriet explained,
"were a cultivated taste" but after a few years, the Wallingford
Community grew and sold nine hundred and fifty bushels of them
in one season, and, after strawberries, she went on, "came rasp-
berries and blackberries, the show harvest of these fruits carrying
the Bees into September; and then came grape-gathering in the
hazy beauty of October."

Less romantic, the winter Bees occupied themselves with
making bags for a factory in Meriden—"the cheapest kind of traveling bags of enameled cloth or carpeting. Long stitches and low
wages was the principle. "I felt like a swindler basting the bottoms
with six or eight stitches as I was told to do, but twenty-five cents
a dozen for making would not allow you to be over-scrupulous.
The bag Bees were held for an hour immediately after dinner and
the whole family joined—the men taking to the thimble as grace-
fully as the women had to the hoe. There was reading the while,
and what with the book and the company and the enthusiasm for
work, the hour was very short," As Harriet added, "Anything in
the line of honest labor was welcomed with enthusiasm."

Another industry in "the line of honest labor" was one
which caused both tears and hilarity. Three times a week during
the season, after-supper Bees were held for putting up horseradish.
The work of washing, scraping, grating and bottling was done by a
combination of hand and machine labor, but, as Harriet wrote,
"these were *pathetic* Bees. The scene in the dining room was lugu-
brious in the extreme. The stinging odor—nay, it was something
more palpable than odor—the exhalation, filled the room and to

compel the tear, onions were nothing in comparison. A desperate boy would sometimes take his pan and bottle and sit out in the frost-biting night rather than bear it." There was a good local market for it, however, and it earned the Community from $20 to $30 a week.

Charlotte Miller, a visitor from Oneida to the sister commune at Wallingford, gives a picture of life in that smaller commune. "In the afternoon a Bee was organized for planting corn in a lot some distance from the house, on the bank of the Quinnipiac. Several of the women went; but, as I did not care about taking a long walk, I stayed behind. As I looked out the window I saw Mr. B. standing on his harrow just below the house, and I concluded to go and join him. After a few turns across the lot, he proposed to fix a seat for me on the harrow, which he did, and for about an hour I rode up and down and across the lot on the harrow while Mr. B. guided his oxen till the piece was finished. At half past four the sisters returned from the Bee. They seemed lively and fresh and in no way fatigued by their afternoon's work. They all said that two or three hours work outdoors did not tire them as much as one hour did, once—that their strength increased by labor; and they certainly evinced this in their looks and actions. They have a fearlessness in respect to the weather and exposure of all kinds that is very desirable."

It was admitted that the Wallingford Community did not pay, so far as money was concerned. The economy of combination held good as between communes and even such a eulogist as Harriet was obliged to admit that if they should all go home to Oneida it would save money. Not only would the general subsistence be cheaper but the added industrial force would make more money in the Oneida industries than in their own. It was, obviously, for other than pecuniary advantages that Wallingford was valued.

Those advantages were, simply, health and education. With all its financial problems, Oneida was able to recognize the real benefit to the health of its members of a change of scene. As Harriet wrote, "communities are essentially domestic. They have much to make them contented with home and they exist only by a certain seclusion from other society. A few businessmen go abroad but the mass of the people have no occasion. Nevertheless, change is healthy, and by this arrangement of two families, widely separated and different in many conditions, the members of the

O.C. get the benefit of change without going away from home."

Wallingford was three hundred miles east and a hundred miles south of Oneida, its winters less rigorous, its total climate milder. Long Island Sound was visible from the top of Mount Tom, so that attractions of the seaside were at hand—at first enjoyed from a tent "set up in a grove close to the breakers." It is surprising that to a born Vermonter, like Harriet, the interminable weeds and stones, the woods and mountains of Connecticut seemed "hard-featured and shaggy-bearded, compared to the smooth-faced land on the Mohawk."

It was not the external scene that drew Harriet's admiration, but the change from a large community to a small one. Between the two it was a choice, as she said, between grace and power; "The evolutions of the smaller family were more graceful; those of the larger, more powerful." The Evening Meetings at Wallingford were easy and conversational, you did not have to raise your voice to be heard. Also, she thought, family affection was more demonstrative in the smaller commune. For another thing, the distances were greater in the Oneida buildings; there was more living upstairs, which made the occasional invalid enjoy living in the old Connecticut farmhouse where they could live on the first floor and get out of doors more easily.

The change was also beneficial to the young people. Since personal influence was more immediate in the small family, boys and girls sent there for a term received more direct attention to their habits and spirits. "They developed strong, earnest characters, habits of order and industry, simplicity and sincerity under the personal influence of the fathers and mothers of this Commune. As a school itself, the W.C. has been invaluable to the mother Community."

By a system of daily journals and reports between the two Communes intimate communication was kept open, as well as a valuable record of events for future reference. Experience, Harriet finished, "has taught us all that the large Commune should have a small one as complement, and in every case, I believe that two are better than one. Duality is the universal law. It is not good that a commune, even, should be alone."

This criticism did not, evidently, set well at Oneida. They commented that it was too soon to reason from one experiment as to the size of the perfect home. To reach the ideal it must be assumed first that the internal harmony was complete. Secondly,

that the means for making the home what it should be were un-
limited. In that case, the mansion should be furnished with eleva-
tors, speaking-tubes, deadened floors and walls, assembly rooms
constructed on scientific principle., etc., etc. Under such conditions, the larger Community could be easy and majestic too, having the grand resources of numbers as well as the cozy quietness of
a select few.

Harriet's report in 1876, it will be noted, is concerned with
"domestic arrangements," with "honest Labor," financial difficulties and, on a more cheerful note, with the advantages of Wallingford as a resort for those at Oneida in need of rest and a change of
scene. Not a word about its religious devotions which, thirty years
before, would have been her first concern.

In 1852 her brother-in-law, John Miller, reported to
Brooklyn a visit to the new Wallingford Commune and his first
care was to investigate the state of their souls. "My first visit to
the Wallingford Community's school was satisfactory and profitable. Their earnest devotion to God—their love of improvement—
their practical faith in the confession of Christ within them, guiding them into all truth, their freedom to employ faithful criticism
as the remedy for the cure of every evil, secures and promotes true
harmony among themselves. And so far as I am able to judge, the
inhabitants of the town are on peaceable and friendly relations
with them. And why should they not be? They are a people who
mind their own business; pay their debts; do not quarrel among
themselves, nor with their neighbors; educate their own children;
teaching them the fear of the Lord; in a word, they are earnestly
endeavoring to know and do the *will of God* in all things."

It would appear that the heirs of Mr. Henry Allen were
doing their best to carry out his wishes.

One is tempted to wish that the *Spiritual Magazine*, the
Free Church Circular, the three *Annual Reports*, or all of them
had given us a little less theology and a little more specific information about the mundane details of those first years after leaving
Putney. We do know something of their financial difficulties:
"Our liabilities are $4,820, our assets, $9,400—but all of it in real
estate. We are at present nearly out of funds." This was reported
by Mr. Cragin in 1848, but somehow John Miller, their treasurer,
never lost faith that the Lord would provide and, time after time,
he did, but often at the last minute which, to the less faithful,
must have been somewhat nerve-wracking.

The *Third Report* records the opening of four "foreign" branches of the Association: one at Newark, New Jersey, which supported itself by a combination of machine shop and jewelry stores; one at Cambridge in northern Vermont, specializing in agriculture; one at Manlius, New York, some twenty-five miles west of Oneida, also supported by agriculture; and, earliest and most important, what they called the Brooklyn Station, located at 43 Willow Place, Brooklyn, in a house formerly owned by Abram Smith.

It seems possible that the Brooklyn branch, together with the other branch communes as they were formed, kept handwritten journals which were sent to headquarters at Oneida for incorporation in the periodical then being published. Unhappily, only the *Brooklyn Journal* for 1849 and, of much later reports, only a portion of those from the years 1879 and 1880 from Wallingford and Oneida have survived. Aside from these and any private diaries and letters still extant, we have only a mass of papers, untranslated, so to speak, since they were transcribed largely in the phonographic symbols which the Community had learned to use. This system of stenography or phonography, as it was called, was devised by a James E. Munson, and it is our misfortune that his method is related neither to the Gregg nor the Pitman nor any other school of shorthand which is in modern use. If, or when, these papers are finally deciphered, we may have a valuable addition to our knowledge of the early days of the Oneida Community.

A collection of yellowed papers in the possession of the Oneida Community Historical Committee is our best and almost only source for details of the Brooklyn Station. They are a typed copy, probably from the collections of George W. Noyes, entitled *The Brooklyn School*, and from internal evidence seem to be a journal kept either by Harriet Holton Noyes or Mary Cragin, or perhaps both. From the opening of this branch, Mr. and Mrs. Noyes and Mr. and Mrs. Cragin lived there "as affording a more quiet place for reflection and a better opportunity to act on the Association than a residence directly in it." It is only a guess that John Humphrey Noyes saw residence in the metropolis as a better chance to bring his theories to public notice than an obscure country commune could afford. In any case, he must have felt sufficiently confident of success to invest some three thousand dollars of the Community's funds in the house next door to the Smith house. This gave them extra accommodation for their printing establishment, from which their paper was published, as well as for entertaining a constant flow of visitors from Oneida and—this seems wildly unlikely—of extending their gold chain manufacturing business.

"This industry," they wrote in the *Third Annual Report* in 1851, "was taken up providentially and in the true enthusiasm of inspiration, and besides contributing pretty liberally to the support of the Brooklyn family through the winter, has given us considerable advance in the solution of industrial problems." This improbable sounding enterprise had apparently been introduced by Mr. Thomas, a jeweler who was a member of the short-lived branch commune at Newark, New Jersey. In 1854, when financial stringency dictated a concentration of forces at Oneida, the Newark station was eliminated and apparently Mr. Thomas and the gold-chain making with it.

Judging by the letters of converts, as printed in the *Spiritual Magazine* and *Free Church Circular*, 1848-50, admirers from a distance and prospective members from nearer by wrote in ecstatic terms. "Revelling in the Halls of the Montezumas is no comparison to me with the privilege of living in a loving community— where we are free to have God wash away all exclusiveness from our natures and teach us to worship Him in beauty and holiness and love. Such a community we have here." This, from a recent joiner.

However, on the same page of the *Spiritual Magazine*, August 5, 1848, the editors were obliged to make a plea—in very small type—for financial aid from their outside friends, "which may have a bearing on their duty to the Kingdom of God." They had made no money by their publications but had spent a large amount of their private funds on them. The capital of the Association was embarassed by liabilities growing out of the persecutions to which they had been subjected. The removal from Putney and the cost of the necessary buildings at Oneida, as well as their subsistence, had cost money. "In view of these facts, let every one whose heart is with us consider faithfully what God would have him do. So long as present good signs are before us, we shall not be discouraged or draw back from the advanced position which we are assuming. But we apprise our friends of the liabilities of that position, that they may share with us the burdens of our common enterprise."

How many of the faithful responded to this plea is one of the mundane facts we should like to know. Income is not mentioned. Out-go is reported in the construction at Oneida of, first, what they called their Mansion House and, later, of a house for the children of the Association, of whom there were then fifty-seven under the age of fifteen years. They planned "other buildings for lecture rooms, work-shops etc., as soon as present engagements will allow." Even more important on the practical side, "Considerable progress has been made toward a self-supporting industrial system, by introducing the different mechanical trades."

This editorial appeared in the *Spiritual Magazine* for August 11, 1849, and was signed JHN, evidently written while he was living in the Brooklyn Commune. It sounded ambitious, but the day-to-day notes of the Brooklyn group record almost nothing in the way of "progress" and show little interest in any "industrial system" or the introduction of any "mechanical trade."

According to the entries in the Brooklyn diary, aside from printing the paper, criticism was their chief preoccupation. The journal of the *Brooklyn School* gives us a glimpse of the spiritual rigors of those days. From week to week, members from Oneida arrived in batches, generally of half a dozen or more, including some children who occasionally presented problems of behavior. They were met with the Community's universal panacea, criticism, sometimes too much of it. On one occasion, John Humphrey Noyes detected "a spirit of criticism with regard to the management of the children" which, he thought, was the result of an influence from without. The person he believed responsible for this "hard, sharp spirit" was advised to turn her attention to the truth about *herself*. He advised all to bring to light anything in their past experience which obstructed their course. They must not be content with a momentary conversion but "must untie all the devil's knots in their past lives."

A few nights later, Mrs. Whitfield was criticized for a spirit of flattery; all worldly love had a spirit of flattery in it. Persons were like lumps of ice put in water. They were only good as they melted into the water; so individuality was good only as it melted into God. On another evening he criticized Mrs. Cragin and Mr. Burnham for carelessness and pleasure-seeking in learning to play on the violin. "This led to an interesting conversation about not being seduced from the truth by a desire to please others." Much was said about vigilance; "that all the difficulties we had been digging into, Millerism, the Canastota Convention, Philena's trouble, came down to this: *I did not think.*" The atmosphere of a city is strongly charged with pleasure-seeking and we must strive to keep our minds chaste and simple."

On the subject of fanaticism Mr. N. said that "a fanatical mind wants a thing to be true and bends everything to it. Sincere faith has a truth-loving liberal marvellousness; fanatical faith, on the other hand, has a wide-open marvellousness and does not question anything." Millerism, he said was "a fortune-telling for the millions."

In criticizing Mr. Abbott, it was said that although he had a spirit of honesty and meant to do right, he was not in partnership with God and the Community. He was like a mouse in his hole; they did not know where he would show himself next. He did not speak or, if he did, he was apt to say something foreign to the subject others were talking about. Mr. A. also had a self-justifying spirit and thought the church did not appreciate him. He must conquer egotism and believe that those whom the Lord put over him knew more than he did.

Mrs. Burt, the wife of Jonathan, at the time when the Putney emigrants first descended upon her, had been what Parker has described as "'recalcitrant and obstinate,' though all hoped for her conversion." She evidently visited Brooklyn and so came in for one of Noyes's searching criticisms. She was, he said, naturally gentle, unassuming, and kind but by her dealings with the New York Perfectionists she had acquired a harsh, hard spirit, of which she would have to repent. "There was still a leak in her spirit which let in worldliness and this leak was connected with her mother." That, as was seen in Maria Clark's case, would draw anybody back into the world. "Maria was once cut off from the world much as a peninsula is from the mainland, but her mother was the isthmus which joined her to the world and now she had gone clear back. We should be islands entirely surrounded by God." Maria had evidently proposed to join the Community but later lost heart and returned to the world.

Some remarks were made to James Baker about his effeminacy and want of good taste. He was advised to associate with Mr. Leonard who had a strong spirit. James had been in the habit of tracing his difficulties back to eating and drinking, but they should be attributed to a weak feminine spirit. He should ask for strength, "be strong in the Lord and in the power of his might. The kingdom of God is not in meat and drink or in abstinence."

A few outside affairs were briefly mentioned. John Miller

arrived from Oneida, via Putney, and gave them an account of what they called "the Putney War" which was a lawsuit brought by their old Putney enemy, Mr. Lamb, whose daughter, Lucinda, had attempted to join the Noyes circle by marrying George Noyes but had been snatched back from what her father considered a fate worse than death and bundled off to relatives in Massachusetts, out of harm's way. Two years later Mr. Lamb was suing George Noyes for having proposed to marry his daughter.

A party of six left for Oneida and two days later seven others arrived from there; Mr. Miller took them all shopping and sight-seeing in the city. One Sunday they went over to Trinity Church where they met the noted Mr. Chandler who later called on them in return and took tea. After he had gone they "had a fine laugh at the coolness of his manner." They thought it would be well not to imitate him. However, two days later Mr. Noyes was invited to dine with Mr. Chandler at the Clinton Hotel and met various other notables, "who all treated him very respectfully." Some weeks later they had another call from Mr. Henry James. He had evidently made a previous call, not recorded. This time they noted that he "was full of controversy."

There were, throughout this period journalized, general discourses by Mr. Noyes on such a variety of subjects as dreams, nicety of thought and precision of thought—"some are more adapted to making outlines, other to filling in details"—treachery to women, philoprogenitiveness, honorable feelings to God and marriage. These, together with almost daily criticism, were a heavy burden upon Mr. Noyes so that one day "he talked with the class about helping him. He said he must stop sending for folks if they drew upon his life in this way. His state was such that he needed a warm, genial atmosphere, instead of which he was surrounded by fear." They all agreed to help him. Mr. Miller began by talking about the similarity of slavery and marriage. After the class left for Oneida, they had a very quiet week and for diversion went to see the launching of three steam vessels. "There was an immense crowd and the vessels were launched beautifully."

Difficulties arose in the Newark Commune concerning the affairs of Mr. William Inslee, a capable machinist whose services the Association wished to retain. Noyes had suggested that Jonathan Burt join the Newark group and work in Inslee's shop. Inslee's brother, who was not a commune member, objected to this and made a counter-proposition to divide the tools of the establishment and let brother William take the basement for his shop.

Not unnaturally, when Mr. Inslee next appeared in Brooklyn he was "rather disheartened and wearied by a quarrel he had had with his brother and wished he could rest. He stayed all night. His head was quite disturbed and he was somewhat afraid he should go crazy but concluded to go home and try again. Mr. Burt followed him in the afternoon and returned Friday with a good report of Mr. Inslee's state." He had evidently recovered sufficiently so that the next week he was able to accompany Mrs. Harriet Noyes and Mrs. Cragin to hear Christy's Minstrels.

Another imbroglio, originating in the Newark commune, concerned the case of a Mr. and Mrs. Lynch who had been fringe members of the Newark group and who now wished to join the Oneida Community. After one preliminary visit, Mr. Thomas and Mr. Inslee had evidently interviewed the couple and brought back a favorable report. The Lynches "offered themselves and their property to the church. They were anxious to get rid of care, and they admitted that Mr. Lynch's business was running down. They had a very interesting conversation in which they traced the providential care of God in their affairs." For some reason this line of argument did not strike either Mr. Thomas or Mr. Inslee as contradictory. They were impressed by the fact that Mrs. Lynch was the first Perfectionist in Newark. It was evident that they needed help and it was thereupon decided that Mr. Abram Smith should be sent for to go into partnership with Mr. Lynch, to keep up the place and recover the business.

Mr. Smith, however, went to Newark with a different idea —that Mr. Lynch and his wife should go to Oneida and that enough of their stock in trade and what land they owned should be sold to pay their debts, or that their house should be sold if the Newark brethren saw fit. To this plan the Lynches consented and it was agreed that they should go to Oneida with their son and grandchild, but two days later Mr. Smith returned from his visit to Newark and reported that he had settled the Lynch business. They had not, after all, given up their property fully and he now left them to their own devices.

This wrangle, plus poor Mr. Inslee's troubles, led the Brooklynites to regard the Newark branch with some mistrust, so that when Mrs. Whitfield's daughter came from New Jersey to visit them she "brought with her the Newark fog. It was a poisonous spirit which made us sleepy and stupid." They told the young woman that if she wished religious instruction they would talk with her, but they did not wish a worldly visit. "She received what we said very coldly. She was obliged to stay all night and had an uncomfortable time. We all went to bed with the headache."

Nothing, beyond the bare mention of its existence, was printed in the *Circular* describing the Community branch colony in Fletcher, northern Vermont. George Cragin wrote in a report of July 1852: "Mr. K— [Kinsley] and family from Oneida had been faithfully laboring since their arrival, the 2nd of June" and went on to report further that a meeting of four families of that place had "pledged themselves, their property and all their possessions to the cause of practical communism, as advocated by John H. Noyes." The house where the meeting took place belonged to Mr. John Kinsley who continued there for some two years as the leader of the small group. This tiny commune strove to support itself by dairy farming but was ultimately closed at the time of the general move for concentration in 1854.

THE WORDENS

THE THIRD ANNUAL REPORT of the Oneida Association exhibiting, as it announced, its progress to February 20, 1851, gives scant attention to the new Station at Manlius, New York, merely mentioning that it had eight members and that "a member of the Association, having a good farm at Manlius which he was prevented from selling by unfavorable circumstances, it was decided to occupy it ourselves. Accordingly, it has been the residence of several families of the Association during the winter."

The only direct report from this new colony is in a letter written sometime during the winter of 1850-51 from its erstwhile owner and now leader, Marcus Worden. He was apparently, over optimistic. "We feel here at Manlius that God's kingdom is come; that the banner of Theocratic government is spread over us. All hearts are turned to the central organization with grateful aspirations of affection and love, while the progressive spirit of truth is guiding our way and urging us forward to greater achievements over self and Satan, and to a brighter union with Christ and each other."

This is all, or almost all, that any publication of the Oneida Community ever recorded either of that farm or the man who had owned it. The owner was M. L. Worden. The farm was eventually sold. The members who had originally left it for the Oneida Community finally seceded. That was the end of it.

But by an extraordinary piece of good fortune, a small trunk, doll-size, covered with worn deerskin and decorated by brass nailheads, came to light a few years ago among my father's possessions and was found to contain what must be most of the letters that M. L. Worden ever received. Most are undated; some are almost illegible, many are extremely personal. Altogether they give us what might be called an inside view of certain of the members and some of the events of the early days of the Manlius Station and later of the second Putney community, described in the next chapter.

If it should appear to the reader that a disproportionate amount of space and detail is allotted to the Worden letters, it must be explained that aside from the scantiest mention of family affairs, most of the chronicle of the Community as it appears in the *Spiritual Magazine*, the *Free Church Circular*, or the early numbers of the Oneida *Circular* relates to the more or less official activities of the group—criticism, financial matters, the progress of their various industrial efforts, the comings and goings between the various branch communes, and, of course, religion. The Worden letters, being private, were personal; not only what people did but what they felt, what they thought, and, quite humanly, a spice of gossip retailed to the absent member. From these details the broad impersonal public picture becomes smaller and more human: more what one would wish to be able to imagine; how it felt to be a member of the Oneida Community in the early days.

Who were the Wordens? The queer little trunk also contained a queer little book entitled *"Some Records of Persons by the Name of Worden, etc. etc."* It was written by a gentleman named O. N. Worden and published by him in Lewisburg, Pennsylvania, in 1868. It is the most naive as well as the worst organized genealogy I have ever seen, but it is crammed with information and, best of all, the several blank pages at the back of the book have been handwritten with quantities of extra facts pertaining to the branch of the family settled in and around Manlius, New York. From it we learn that the original Worden immigrants from Scotland reached this country in 1635 or 1636 and settled and proliferated in the New England States, mostly Massachusetts, Connecticut, and Rhode Island. Gradually, as the centuries rolled on, some of them moved to New York State and other states farther west.

The branch of the Worden family with which we have to do is the issue of Major Walter Worden, an officer under Colonel Hopping in the War of 1812, who afterwards "died of dropsy of the brain." Of his family of ten children, M. Lafayette, as he is designated in the genealogy, was the sixth son. Of how the family property descended to him there is no information. He was born in 1813, married Mary Catherine Cook from Stone Arabia, New York, in 1839, by whom he had three daughters—Harriet, Cornelia, and Susan—buried Mary in 1848, and joined the Oneida Community in 1849.

Whether his parents had simply run out of names—this boy was the seventh child—or whether they were inspired by the visit of the famous French hero who stopped off at Syracuse to see the opening of the Erie Canal in 1825, is not known. The fact remains that this boy who, in that year, must have been twelve years old, was, for whatever reason, named Marquis de Lafayette—the whole thing, title and all. For the rest of his life he was called mostly Marquis which naturally degenerated into Marcus, although for many years he did sign his letters "M.Lafayette." (The family seemed to have run to remarkable names; in one branch there were sons named America and Liberty).

Marquis's younger brother, Leander, with his wife Keziah and two children, had joined the Oneida Association in November 1848. Marcus, perhaps less impulsive, did not join at that time but sent his eldest daughter, Harriet, to Oneida in January, 1849. I cannot imagine, however, that any conventional prejudices held him back. He had previously been an enthusiastic member of other radical groups and was sociable, gregarious, naive, and a natural joiner. Judging from his correspondence and the stories handed down in the family—he was my father's maternal grandfather—he was a quaint, gentle, and original man, and joining a strange and exotic cult was perfectly in character.

His letter of application for Harriet sounds extremely devout: "In the name and for the sake of Christ," but he, himself, apparently hesitated, although both George and Mary Cragin for the Community wrote him cordially about the reception of nine-year-old Harriet. Marcus, however, did not immediately join. It may be that a letter from Jonathan Burt, a leading member at Oneida, who did not mince matters, damped his ardor.

"You ask for advice about your property and your children. If we were disposed to accept jurisdiction over foren property under any circumstances, your vaselating, undecided state would forbid us to do so in the present case. I would say to you, how long halt ye between two opinions? We believe most ashuredly that God is not straitened concerning any person in that condition. He can do without them if they can do without him. If you doubt the correctness of our claim to being the Kingdom of God, then I say, settle in your mind to stay where you are in isolation until you are satisfied concerning us. We do not ask you to receive our testimony. We tell you frankly that we have no time nor strength to expend upon such subjects. With regard to Harriet, we have made up our minds that she shall be left either wholly under the influence of wordly society or wholly under our care."

Mr. Cragin used a kinder tone, on May 6, 1849: "We are not called to negotiate with anyone but if you find, on acquaintance with God, that it is his will that you should come here, feel free to come."

At this point Worden must have written asking that Mr. Noyes come to Manlius to discuss the matter. Mr. Burt wrote that this was impossible. He also replied to what may have been Worden's objections to giving up his farm: "What we wish to say is not that we want the deed to your farm or the money it will procure, but we want a proof of you that you will stand the test of trial. I

Marquis de Lafayette (Marcus) Worden, was in charge of the Manlius branch commune and, later, the second Putney commune.

will advise you, do not come here under circumstances which are certain to secure results so disastrous to yourself and us. We want your company but we want it only under circumstances which will secure to you with us the crown of unfading love." (Mr. Burt was always eloquent but his spelling must be seen to be believed. These are verbatim extracts from his letter.)

What happened next is recorded only in two unexplained and perplexing happenings. In the Community's *Record of Secessions and Deaths*, M. L. Worden's name appears as having joined the Association on June 2, 1849. In the *Worden Family Record*, in Marcus' own hand, written in the back of the book, he inscribed as his second wife the name of "Mrs. Sophia Dunn, of Bakersfield, Vt., married at O.C., June 2, 1849." From the Oneida Community *Family Record* we find that Mrs. Sophia Dunn, a widow with three children—Leonard, Julia and Fidelia—joined the Oneida Community on October 23, 1848. Apparently she married Marquis de Lafayette Worden seven months after her arrival at O.C., but on the very first day when he had finally made up his mind and joined the Community. There is no evidence that he had ever known the lady before this date or why the marriage was coincident with *his* membership—but not with *hers*.

Whether, as two historians of the Putney commune have suggested, John Noyes required the new member to seal his union with the Community by taking one of its members to wife—which would seem illogical, considering his disapproval of the world's marriage—or whether there was some legal reason, perhaps connected with Worden's property or his children, cannot be known.

A letter dated August 29, 1849, written in Worden's hand and addressed to his new wife, suggests that this was a marriage in name only, but does not explain why it happened:

You say I am a trial to you on account of special claiming etc., Now I have confessed that I have not willingly or knowingly caused such trial or suffering. And further I am frank to say that if you are brot into suffering on account of your connection with me —and that connection a *mere formal or legal affair*— [emphasis added] I should say it is best to dissolve such a connection. I will not tenaciously adhere to it or any other like legal or formal transaction which shall in its operation procure the misfortune of yourself or any other person. If my marriage relation shall be deemed the

procuring cause of such jurisdiction over me, than I shall beg leave to
dissent from such opinion or relationship.

Believing that such is not the order of true marriage relations between husband and wife, as brought to view in the New
Testament.

M. La Fayette

to Mrs. Worden.

There is only one communication from Mrs. Worden, written nearly a year later, which bears out the impression conveyed
by her husband that married life in the Community, even if only
a formal affair, presented difficulties. Dated February 25, 1850,
it reads:

> Dear Brother:
> Having a desire to be faithful to you and to God, I thought
> I would mention frequent complaints made of you from the women.
> They say they are very much annoyed by the habit you have of
> catching hold of them when in your company. As I know you wish
> to be a gentleman in every way, I thought I would show my love for
> you by telling you of a fault that hinders your being attractive. True
> love doth not behave itself unseemly. From your sincere sister,
> Sophia Worden.

In a number of reports of Community criticisms of Worden
at this time, Marcus was warned about the encroachment of the
spirit of New York Perfectionism, with which he had previously
been associated. This the Oneida Perfectionists violently disapproved of. The New York Perfectionists were supposed to be antinomian—the heresy that faith alone, exclusive of moral law, was
sufficient to attain salvation—and Free Lovers. Whether this influence was responsible for Marcus Worden's unseemly behavior, if it
was unseemly, can only be guessed. Judging from a large number
of letters from Community women to Worden, written then and
later, it might rather be assumed that he was extremely attractive
to them, which of course could be what motivated Sophia's letter.
Harriet Skinner, John Humphrey Noyes's sister, advised Marcus on
the subject. "I am glad that the effect of your love is to make you
thankful, but I know there are a great many dangers in free love

experience, and as you are comparatively a novice, I want you to make a confidant of Mr. Hamilton and let him instruct you."

In another note, written in July 1850, Harriet perhaps explains Sophia's feelings. "I thought Mrs. Worden had the real 'Marriage spirit' and we did not want to give that spirit any excuse for complaint. We did not need to because we were happy any way. I know that we have a perfect right to freedom, and have no disposition to indulge that spirit in her, but if we give it no food for complaint, perhaps that will be the quickest cure. I should avoid much explanation of any kind—occupy ourselves with the things which be Jesus Christ."

Although written confirmation has yet to be discovered, it has been suggested that the "scandalized whispers" that Parker speaks of as culminating in the 1850 complaints about the Community to the authorities in both Oneida and Madison Counties were threatening enough so that the Association took the precaution of marrying off new joiners as a concomitance to membership. Worden's letter to his wife calls "that connection a mere formal or legal affair," which seems to bear out this theory, and the purport of the letter is to warn his wife not to claim "such jurisdiction" over him. Harriet Skinner's letter to him speaks of Mrs. Worden's "marriage spirit," and urges Marcus not to give her cause for complaint.

The conclusion of this unfortunate union came nearly two years later. Worden, after a nine-months' effort to make a go of a branch commune on his farm at Manlius in the winter of 1850-51, was appointed head of a small group which made a daring return to Putney in the fall of 1851. Apparently Sophia accompanied him into what may have been at first a hostile environment. Whether this affected her health adversely is not known, except that it was presently reported to Oneida that she was ill, probably insane.

However it was, the poor woman died and was buried in Putney, and what is evidently a copy of the inscription on her gravestone is written in an elegant hand on a piece of blue paper. "Sophia A. Dunn, wife of M. LaFayette Worden and a member of the Oneida Community. Born in Bakersfield, Vt., Oct. 9, 1810, Died January 30, 1852. Blessed are they that do his commandments, that they may have right to the tree of life."

The curious postscript to this sad little story is that on the reverse side of the blue paper is pencilled a message, to whom is not indicated, but probably written by Marcus Worden. "My primary object in writing these lines to you is to find out the points of common interest and cooperation that lie between us and see what mutual improvement can be made. Perhaps you may assume that distance and the lapse of time have obliterated all that ever subsisted in our relations and so each is absolved. Here is where it is very important to know the truth and understand the mind of God and his way of doing things and how we may be certain what God means and what he determines shall be executed—that he is faithful on his side to any covenant he makes and though we believe not, yet he will surely perform and the thing must be done according to his will."

The reference to "distance and the lapse of time" suggests that the person addressed was a member of the Oneida group and that "all that ever subsisted in our relations" might mean an unsanctioned "special love" that took place two years before. Unfortunately, our curiosity on this point is not satisfied by anything in the voluminous letters from Mr. Worden's lady correspondents.

Mr. Henry Thayer, an Oneida member who must have been staying in Manlius, on his return to Oneida wrote to Marcus an account of his ride home with little Susan, Worden's four-year-old daughter, who wept and did not want to sit on his lap but was finally consoled and "appeared to enjoy the ride very much." Henry Seymour, another Oneidan, who seems to have been second-in-command to Worden in the little Manlius community, wrote from Oneida to which he had returned for a visit, to "Dear Manlius Friends," that he would be glad of a criticism "if his case demanded it." The criticism came the next morning and, he wrote, "made me feel pretty small, but then I thanked God and prayed that I might be smaller and stay so."

He also reported a discussion of the case of Wallace Worden, Brother Leander's refractory son. Wallace's parents also were criticized and it was thought that the root of the mischief in the boy was in his parents. The result was a most searching criticism which "gave proof of the fact that those who are silent and cold, having no public spirit, invariably have something covered." This could scarcely have applied to Leander who, judging by his letters, was only too warm and voluble, but Keziah, his wife, like her son, Wallace, was a problem the Community never solved.

At this time some kind of altercation was certainly going on at the new commune at Manlius. As early as January 1851 there is mention of the possibility of selling the property in the spring. On October 31, 1850, a six-page paper under the heading "Manlius Affairs," although not in his hand, may have been dictated by John Humphrey Noyes. It does not specify the difficulty except to say that "there is an irritation going on between the leading characters of the Association." Fortunately, Mr. Hamilton and Mr. Burt, who were in charge at Oneida in Mr. Noyes's absence, came down upon the difficulty with sufficient persuasive force toward both parties, probably Mr. Worden and Mr. Seymour, to remove the dissension.

Besides the difficulty with Mr. Seymour, which the good offices of the Central Members, plus the eloquent advice from Mr. Noyes must have dealt with successfuly, there may have been another spot of bother connected with Henry Seymour's wife, Tryphena Seymour, who, as Harriet Skinner wrote to Mr. Worden, was "laboring under the spirit of diseased egotism, pride and love of attention." Mr. Noyes's advice in this case was to let her entirely alone. It appears from this letter that Mr. and Mrs. Skinner had for a time been part of the Manlius group, and after they left, Harriet writes from Oneida that it seemed best for them not to return to Manlius in order to "starve Tryphena into submission to Henry, to give her the real prodigal son's spirit toward the Association so that she will be glad to come here and be a servant instead of wanting to be served." She adds that the Association "expects to withdraw entirely from Manlius before very long and I think that things will go better there without us. Anything that withdraws attention from Tryphena will shorten her captivity to this hateful spirit."

Exactly what the Tryphena difficulty was and whether Marcus Worden was involved in it remains a mystery. Whatever her illness or bad spirit was, Henry Seymour, her husband, was naturally involved in it. Harriet Skinner wrote playfully that "if Henry had thrown his pail of water on to Tryphena instead of giving her a drink in her fainting fit, it would have been just the thing." Among Worden's papers is a sort of envelop marked Tryphena, but it is empty. How he dealt with the problem until the closing of the Manlius branch in the spring and whether Tryphena went back to Oneida and lived there or in one of the other branches until she died in 1877, we do not know.

It is ironic that two such peaceable men as the Worden brothers should be pursued by furies. In early March, before Marcus could shut up shop in Manlius and move back to Oneida, he got news of the trouble Leander was facing at Oneida. Mr. Cragin wrote him about the state of Keziah Worden:

> Ever since the move was made in separating the disobedient from the obedient and devoting the White House to the former class, we have been looking and hoping for some satisfactory change in Keziah but we have not seen the first evidence of repentence and sincerity.
>
> The truth is that she has been the representative of York State Perfectionism in its most subtle form—as active missionary of Satan in disseminating all the evil influences that grow out of *Antinomianism, Charles Weldism, Universalism, etc. etc.* The question came up what good work she has done since she has been a member of this Community, and instead of finding one in any shape or a single act of faith, she has been an active unbeliever, a hiding-place and refuge for every disobedient spirit we have had to deal with. She has been presumptive enough to declare her want of confidence in the Association, at the same time claiming fellowship with Mr. Noyes. Leander is just getting his eyes opened to the fact that she *is* and *has always been*, a very willful woman. She has been an active seducer of men and women. Leander has always been a complete victim of her *fascinations*.
>
> The Community are prepared to make an example in her case as they have in others, and require her whole family to leave the Association on her account. Our confidence in Leander is constantly increasing. We feel a vital union with him and whatever course God may direct us to take in separating her spirit from the body and union with Leander, will not be distrusted.

This is all very surprising since, a year before, both Leander and Keziah, in a letter dated March 28, 1849, from Oneida, speak enthusiastically of the place. Leander reports that "every member made the sollum pledge (at our meeting) of our lives, property, wives, children, husband, fathers, mothers, brothers, sisters and souls—life or death, in persecution or distress, to God and the principles advanced by Mr. Noice and I must say that my heart has not been more rejoiced at any move since I have been here. I have fully and eternally made up my mind that there is no half-way business in this matter."

Keziah's spelling was even worse than her husband's, but her spirit seemed equally devoted: "This is trueley the school of

Leander and Keziah Worden joined the Oneida Community in 1848 and, after much trouble, seceded in 1855.

Christ and the pupels are going through a disiplen that will prepare them for the final consomation of all things, that is, the hay, wood and stubbel and all things that are combustabul in our most sever trials we recogrise the hand of God so that we pray without seesing." To her sister-in-law, Hannah, in Manlius, she wrote that "we are happy in doing the will of God. Our time is very agreeably spent in study and reflection." Not, one must assume, a hard worker.

The next letter from Mr. Cragin advises Marcus that Mr. Noyes wished the matter of selling the farm be "left to us financial characters." He was in favor of selling the farm at a low price, $2,200 in cash. Apparently the Community's excommunication of Leander's family had been carried out, for he says, "In relation to Keziah, I do not wish her to return to the Community until you and the Central members are fully satisfied of her honesty and sincerity." He thought Leander "patriotic enough" not to carry her back until then, "even if he is obliged to return to isolated life and remain there." Leander, he said, should consider this experience invaluable, "just the school to cultivate in him a *manly* spirit that he very much needs."

Several letters dated March and April 1851 deal largely with financial matters in relation to selling the farm. No definite date is given for the actual closing of the commune at Manlius. An undated letter from Harriet Skinner mentions for the first time the "newspaper war which has caused rather a hard run in spirit with all of us, but it appears to brighten up some." Whether this refers to the attack by the District Attorney at Utica in 1851 which resulted in the summons and forced testimony before the Grand Jury, or to the purely verbal attack by the *New York Observer* in 1851-52 which resulted in a temporary moratorium of their social theory, is not clear. Since Harriet adds that Mr. Reynolds "has now gone to Oneida to spend a few weeks to prepare himself for a witness in the case of J. H. Noyes versus public opinion" it would seem likely that she was writing from Brooklyn, in which case the reference would be to the *Observer* affair, and the date would be 1852.

The first definitely dated letter to Marcus Worden was from his brother Leander from Oneida, November 19, 1851, and placed Marcus in Putney, apparently as the responsible head of the little colony which had reopened in the old Noyes home. What actually happened there during the early days of this return engagement between the Noyes Perfectionists and the village worthies who had driven them out of Putney only four years before is not recorded. Leander writes his brother, "I think you have borne them with a great deal of courage and forbearance. I am happy to hear of your success in maintaining peace and quietness in the heat of battle. From reports I think you must have a very happy community."

One gathers from his letter that Leander is more than ever a convinced communist—"The evidence grows brighter in my mind that Mr. Noyes is the touching point between heaven and earth." He had apparently returned to Oneida, and Keziah, in a reformed state, was with him. "Keziah returned last Saturday quite brite and happy and brings a favorable report." Another letter, also from Oneida, dated February 1852, condoles with his brother on the death of his wife, Sophia. After this there is nothing else until August, when he wrote from Manlius in rather a gloomy key: "I have been troubled of late with my besetting temptation of accusation and self-condemnation. At a time when the perception is clear and the heart joyful and happy, a little circumstance transpires which changes the whole of life into a dark and gloomy state." What was troubling him he does not reveal. The rest of the letter deals mainly with the Manlius relatives until, at the end, he writes, "I think I should be much more free to write if I could forget myself and the individual responsibilities that thrust themselves upon me almost continually in regard to Wallace and many other things."

The saga of poor Leander dragged along until he finally left the Community in 1855 and continues thereafter for twenty years in a long series of pathetic letters to his older brother, Marcus. He "lacked manliness; he needed to gather pluck; he vaselated," as Mr. Burt wrote him in the very beginning. Keziah, his wife, was certainly the dominant member and he could never escape her. He had fathered a son in his last year at Oneida— naturally "an accident," given Leander's talent for failure—and managed to get into a quarrel with the child's mother and her husband. He tried, time after time, to be a "pedler" as he wrote Marcus, but it seemed that each time he started out his health gave way; he got sick fifteen miles from home and was obliged to return with empty pockets.

One Sunday morning in 1854 he was summoned to the Reception Room of the Mansion House, where a committee of eight was assembled to discuss the wrongdoings of his son Wallace, who, they told him, "was guilty of licentious actions and very foul talk with the children." After this there was some plain talk, the burden of which "fell on Keziah as it always has, for having a loose, licentious spirit which was to blame for Wallace's diabolical spirit." The advice of the committee was that he should take Wallace back into the world and search out the cause of the evil. They added that this would be just the discipline Leander needed to put pluck into him. They also criticized both Leander and Keziah for failure to carry out the Social Theory.

Leander took his criticism meekly. But what should he do, he wrote Marcus; what course to take; where to go? He writes sadly that if his family were not worthy to be counted as one with the Community, he wanted to know it, "that I may know what my destiny is to be."

The date given in the Oneida Community records for the "secession" of Leander and family is February 1855, although it appears from a letter Leander wrote on March 4 of that year that, while his family was to remain at Manlius, he, himself, planned to return to Oneida. His letter to Marcus found him "again pleasantly seated in the parlor at dear old Oneida." He had left Manlius "after another storm and contention with the old family spirit," brought about, not unnaturally, by a "proposition I made to Keziah that I would give her a clearance from me so that she could get married again if she chose, and that she might have control of Wallace on condition that she would release all claim on [his daughter] Thecla and let her go with me." There was a lot more "storm and contention" and "one thing after another came up till we had quite a time." His mother and sister joined in, begging him to leave the Community and "settle down to take comfort with his family," and Keziah even offered to help him form a new community on the farm. In the end, they agreed on nothing and Leander took his leave, "feeling more undesided than ever."

Correspondence for the rest of that year between Leander and Marcus dealt mainly with his efforts to regain fellowship with the Oneida group and his even less successful efforts at peddling. Marcus was apparently sympathetic and once or twice sent him small amounts of money. By 1856 his peddling was actually looking up, but the situation at home was not pleasant and he toyed with the idea of going west with a Worden relative who was leaving for Kansas. As usual, Leander vacillated, considered moving to Putney, thought he might try shoe-making, wondered if he should buy a farm. As he wrote his brother, "I feel loose in regard to most everything."

The correspondence went on and on, all letters saved by Marcus until 1875 when he, too, had seceded and the Oneida

Community was a thing of the past for both of them except that Marcus still had three daughters, now grown women, living there. Both brothers had moved to Vineland, New Jersey, where they spent the rest of their lives.

THE SECOND PUTNEY COMMUNE

THE REPOSSESSION of their old home in Putney by the Oneida Communists in the autumn of 1851 was a daring move and one justified by its success. Marcus Worden, his wife, and one other couple were the first to make the move into one of the houses of the Noyes property in the town. Other Oneidans followed them. In December 1851, John R. Miller, the leading member at Oneida during John Noyes's absence in Brooklyn, wrote a report of the situation which was published in the *Circular:*

> As it is generally understood that we were driven out of Putney, Vt., in 1847, by public hostilities and compelled to seek a location elsewhere, I think it right that your readers should know the changes which have taken place during the last four years. Prosecutions were commenced against us by three different individuals, who no doubt were instigated by the prevailing spirit to take advantage of the general storm to extract money from us. All manner of falsehoods were put in circulation about us. [But] a great change has come over the spirit of the place.
>
> . . . I find that it is generally supposed that we have sold out our property in Putney and have entirely abandoned the town. This is not so, but quite the contrary. We still own a good farm of 200 acres, which cost $7000; six dwelling houses, a store, chapel, printing office and a grist mill, besides other property; making in all not less than $15,000.
>
> . . . The two families from Oneida have lived there nearly three months with their principles well understood . . . are well treated and apparently respected by the best part of the community.

> Now, after four years, we are, apparently at liberty to take posses-
> sion of our property again. . . . If this is not so, and the spirit of the
> Inquisition still reigns there, I call on the people to express it be-
> fore we go further. Unless this is done, we shall take it for granted
> that they have retracted the movements of 1847, and shall act
> accordingly.

There is no record that this challenge was ever taken up by
the general populace of Putney, although an occasional unforgiving
character gave Marcus Worden a few bad moments. As he wrote to
"dear Brooklyn Friends,"

> I appreciate the kind and respectful treatment I have re-
> ceived in this place, with one exception.
> There is a man by the name of Keyes, with whom I had
> never spoken before, who, as I went into the Post Office on two oc-
> casions, assailed me with violent taunts for my connection with Per-
> fectionists. As I had given him no cause or provocation for this
> abuse, and had otherwise been well-treated, this attack was very un-
> expected, as well as uncourteous. Perceiving that he had a spirit of
> animosity and bitterness, I refrained from any argument, desiring
> the spirit of Christ manifested when he suffered wrong. Since then I
> have met with nothing disagreeable from him or anyone else; but
> general mutual good feeling seems to subsist between us and all our
> customers and any with whom we have intercourse.

A correspondent from Putney shattered this pleasant illusion in the *Circular* 1851: "There was a meeting held and led in its
deliberations by *Israel Keyes* [who] made some pathetic appeals
on behalf of the young that a stop should be put to the return of
this great corrupting evil and heresy—*Perfectionism*. . . . We cannot
learn what organization was adopted except to appoint a committee of two, to take such measures as they should deem expedient."

The *Circular* commented ironically: "We were aware that
Israel Keyes did not like our late arrangement for reoccupying our
homestead at Putney. But the expressions of good feeling which
Mr. Miller met with among the *people* of Putney induced him to
think that Israel Keyes might not be the whole of Putney. . . . It
was thought that the Gentiles of Putney might have a voice in the
disposal of the town. . . . If we are mistaken in this and if Israel
still remains the autocrat and true representative of all nations in

the Putney world, we shall cheerfully retire before him, given fair notice, and wait for the advent of republicanism. But we fear he will have to stop the mails and break up the railroads before he will possess his kingdom in peace."

There is no report of further activities of his group or its committee or of any other unpleasantness in Putney in the rest of the 1850-51 volume of the *Circular*, so one presumes that Mr. Keyes and his cohorts subsided without further action.

The rest of Worden's papers on the second Putney commune consisted in various letters, mostly from Oneida friends and personal notes, often scribbled by him as *aide-memoire* for the composition of his so-called Log, a sort of diary in which he faithfully recorded the activities of himself and the other members of his little flock.

One, dated January 1850, is a kind of confession by Worden: "I have experienced evil from excesses of alimentiveness. Have been very sensible at times of obstructing and, I might say, of destroying my spiritual action in my heart by yielding to a propensity for eating and drinking and, after a heavy meal, find my vision obtuse and my whole spiritual energy impaired. And I think I can now see that such obstructions are the counter-action of Sensuality, through the channel which is not subdued to spiritual control.

"And I know on the contrary that abstinence has much increased my facilities in both mental and spiritual progress—and that deep and earnest inspired exercise of my mind has been the power by which this unsanctified action of alimentiveness has been at times under control and hence I think our hope of overcoming is based entirely on the supreme rule of divine life in us—that Christ here shall be exalted as 'Prince and Savior' in this department, and I believe the torments growing out of unsanctified amativeness have found there their support and will here find their doom."

The next letter from Marcus appeared in the *Circular* for February 8, 1852. It was written from Putney and reported the death of his wife, Sophia: "Dear Friends, I write to you under the affecting circumstance not to say, afflictive. No, I will not, I cannot, complain of the dealings of our heavenly Father. 'He doeth all things well.' My heart does feel on this occasion and my feeling is that God has come nigh us. Neither do we mourn as those without hope. We have hope, not only for ourselves but for her who is now absent; absent in body, yet present in spirit. The recollection of the meek submissiveness of her last hours etc etc. Satan, the accusser, had taken advantage of all her weaknesses. She was carried to the desperation of insanity under his oppression. But as the flesh sunk, the spirit rose. Hope, faith and charity reign in our little circle." A note below this letter says that G. W. Noyes and S. R. Leonard went to Putney to assist in the last services for the dead. They brought a good report from their friends there.

A letter of condolence from a friend in Massachusetts links this death with that of Mary Cragin of sacred memory and remarks that now Hades seemed to have lost its gloom. She also mentions that "The Spirits" were beginning to manifest themselves in her locality by "writing, rapping, tipping and other common forms of trying to make the acquaintance of the dwellers in the flesh" but her family had avoided this bustle and excitement.

Another letter was written in a minute hand by Mrs. Burgess, a woman who had been appointed "Mother" to Marcus' eldest daughter Harriet, then living in the Brooklyn commune and who was apparently making heavy weather of it. Harriet, she reported, was enveloped in a superficial spirit. "She would make great pretentions and confessions while the fogg of insincerity was thick." She had also, out of pure mischief, scattered some of the *Circular*'s type about the house and then lied about it. However, just as Mrs. Burgess was losing the last ray of hope, "God enabled Harriet's footstep to be a little lighter, her eye a little milder and finally an earnestness commenced which improved her appearance very much" (Harriet was then twelve years old; it is difficult not to sympathize with her "fogg of insincerity").

A letter from John Skinner dated June 13, 1852, thanks Marcus for paying a visit to the old Skinner homestead in Westmoreland, New Hampshire, and in the course of the letter gives an account of his own rather alarming family. One brother, Dolphus, had apparently circulated an "appeal" ("so abusive toward our association") two years before and managed to get it signed by all but one of his brothers. These others, less violently opposed to the Community than Dolphus, were now apparently softening toward John Skinner; one had come to visit him, others had written apologizing, another had presented the errant brother with a three-volume *Documentary History of New York State* and sundry other books which had come his way when he was a member of the Senate. New England seemed to be repenting its tar and feathers.

Two letters from John R. Miller sounded a more realistic note of caution. In the first he wrote: "I felt, in reading a note that George H. wrote, that he and Helen would need a little *caution.* They must remember that they are on the old battle field where all their actions are watched. They must remember that they are in a gossiping New England village, where everything is seen through a magnifying glass when looking at us. We have been growing in favor with all the people there because we have walked wisely before them. We don't want a more pleasing spirit but we want to walk by inspiration. If we please God I have no fear of the people. Let them see that they 'avoid the appearance of evil.' I don't know how much occasion there is for this advice, but I couldn't satisfy my own conscience without giving it. I don't want to check any proper liberty in them, but I want they should seek the public interest before personal pleasure."

The second letter apparently refers to the threat of the Utica District Attorney. It is dated July 19, 1852, which could date that outrageous affair before the Grand Jury as possibly occurring in early 1852 or late 1851 instead of 1850, as Parker states in *A Yankee Saint* (p. 188).

The letter says, in part: "you may be sure that you are all remembered with sincere love. *If we should be obliged to scatter—* and it is quite possible we may—I doubt not we should find a quiet home for some of our folks in Putney. We hardly think of a dispersion except when our attention is called to the subject by letters from the other stations."

A letter to Marcus, from Mr. Cragin, dated Brooklyn, October 17, 1852, makes no reference to such a dispersion but writes "in a spirit of light . . . that does not fear criticism but loves it as our best friend." He then proceeds to be perfectly frank with them all: "My prevailing impression in regard to the Putney Church is that there is a *morbid, sickly* spirit in some way connected with your *amativeness.* Such a spirit is uneasy, desiring *outward gratification,* a craving appetite, but *unhealthy.*

"If this spirit, such as I have criticized in Mr. W., is allowed to work unrebuked, it will destroy the working of true love. I do not wish to criticize anyone in particular, as this enemy is a *principality*—a subtle spirit attempting to abuse and destroy all healthy action in love. I think so much of true love and *true, healthy expression of true love* that it makes me suspicious of all imitations of it. But in order to detect the false from the true, we must have an *earnest, deep* prayer constantly in our hearts for spiritual union with Christ and the Church above—a union that will give us true peace and satisfaction of heart. 'Be sober, be diligent, because your adversary, the devil, as a roaring lion, walketh about seeking whom he may devour; whom resist steadfast in the faith.'"

It would appear that Mr. Cragin had been visiting the Putney station—hence these fears. A week later he wrote again expressing his gratitude that his recent communication was "so heartily accepted." He felt no anxiety, he writes, regarding the result of his letter, but one is permitted to wonder, since he goes on to say that "the reports that have been sent you within a few days will, I have no doubt, be sufficient to set things right among you." What was wrong he does not specify.

A number of undated letters from persons—mostly women —who had been living in the Putney commune but had recently returned to Oneida, give bits of description of both places, presumably in 1850-51. One woman wrote, "I have moved into the upper tent room and sleep with Harriet [Marcus Worden's elder daughter] which will, sometimes I presume, remind me of her father, if nothing else does. I have no fears, however, of our forgetting Putney. Very many pleasant remembrances will ever be connected with my stay there and I thank God that distance nor time cannot separate hearts that are made one by union with Christ. It would make Ann Eliza's eyes sparkle, I reckon, to hear the music of the band. Mrs. Ackley, too, would not be wholly indifferent. Philena and Harriet Worden occupy quite a prominent place with them. Everything outwardly seems about as it did a year ago; bag Bees, Bible game and working are the same with little alteration."

Another letter from an Oneida woman mentions the Putney Journal which Worden was sending to Oneida: "I feel indebted to you for your journals. You certainly have taken a real deal of pains. A daily journal like yours helps me to look in on you and enjoy the side view amazingly. How do you get along dancing? Do you practice it often? I have half a mind to write off for you two or three figures that we have been learning here." How we wish that she had done so! She ends the letter by asking Mr. Worden to buy her a yard and a half of "muslin delaine like my dress, to make a sack of. We are all agreeing to dress very warm this winter and so dispense with less heat from the stoves."

Other bits and pieces written from Putney to Oneida help to make a picture of life in the Putney Community. "Samuel cracked some butternuts for supper, which was an unexpected treat. We commenced reading *Rob Roy* tonight. Hial put up two bedsteads for Oneida and helped to put down the carpet in the middle room. Louisa doing various things. Ellen tending the milk and butter, Lady Noyes [mother of John Humphrey Noyes] helps a little about her room and is writing. A Bee in the afternoon setting out strawberries. It being my evening to entertain the meeting, I selected the Home Talk, 'A Definite Purpose for All.'"

At a slightly later date—March 1855—four pages of what Marcus Worden called his Log give us some detail of life in the small Putney Commune but perhaps even more of a glimpse into the feelings of an early communist.

M.L. Woarden's Log. March 10, 1855

It is somewhat difficult for me to post up at night *all* the events of the day, but I will try to describe some of the acts and thoughts of today. I was not asleep at midnight or the beginning of the day and did not sleep so sound but that I heard the clock strike every hour except four to six, so I had intervals of sleep, of dreams and of reflection—dreams more or less confused and distracting, thought and reflections more or less spiritual and edifying.

Was awake and arose at first bell—had time to read some in the Bible before breakfast. Was chosen with Jane to read in the game. The game was orderly and pleasant and pretty well executed. After breakfast and answering the inquiries of several and consulting about various little matters of business, etc., we conversed with Mr. and Mrs. [Lyvere? illegible] touching their state. It had the effect to stir me against unbelief and its wicked work.

I then walked to the Depot to see Mr. Pierce, found it rather cold and windy, got little satisfaction about the business with Mr. Pierce. Felt that the world is a cold sphere, attended with disappointment and vexation. Came up to the store and made a small purchase and saw more to make me thankful for community life in contrast with the spirit of the world there. Came home, felt like retirement and interior meditation and read the Bible till dinner.

After dinner sat down and read and found myself soon growing sleepy but resisted it and soon came out to the Braiding Bee.

Practiced splicing for the first time with tolerable success. After braiding, attended wood Bee for an hour or so, then went over to the Blacksmith shop. Mr. Willard agreed to come to the Mill at 7 o'clock in the eve and settle to take up some notes against them. Returned home, soon went out again to the store on an errand for the women. Got the *Circular*, read some in it before supper. After supper and dish-washing (I helped Mrs. Langstaff at the knives) I read and wrote some, then class time, but was called to go to the mill. Settled the acct. of $53.44 for Blacksmithing. Gave up two notes of $71.57 and Rcd. $18.13 in cash.

Felt glad it was not necessary to deal much with the world, but that our community were increasing and destined to meet all wants and save all complicated accts. and are pleasant intercourse. Meeting at 7 and one-half concluded with spelling from dictionary. Some thoughts about dead works, and some talk about the power of habit, with a desire in my mind to live and move by inspiration and break loose from all habits.

The next entry was dated March 13, 1855:

Tho I was not so wakeful as the night before, yet I had quite a nocturnal experience. Was troubled with a distressing cramp in my right leg, mainly below the knee. Had several attacks, the worst was between 3 and 4. Was waked out of sleep by the intruder and had sharp contention for towards one hour. Was obliged to rise up in bed, at the hazzard of disturbing George (my companion) and finally on to my feet and as the clock struck four got relief.

In the midst of this possession I felt in my heart to cry unto the Lord for help and willfully confessed Christ against it. I even came near saying aloud I confess Christ my life and a victorious Savior from this attack of evil, and I felt sudden relief at that moment but it returned again with a spirit that seemed to say now will you confess Christ when you are as badly pained and cramped as ever? And my response was that tho' he slay me yet will I trust him, and nerved my spirit to endure without murmuring, and it seemed that after a little trial of my faith and patience, it all left and I fell asleep in the feeling of satisfaction and thankfulness.

Arose at 6, on ringing of the first bell. Ate breakfast, read again for Bible Game. After Game, read, conversed and various things till noon. Then ate luncheon of cake and apple. Enjoyed that, but had some controversy with the claims of my appetite for a fuller meal. Succeeded in putting it down and felt the better for it.

At one, attended Braiding Bee. Was edified by the reading

and had some new experience in braiding a double turn, but succeeded in doing it slowly. Felt some contest but finally a victory over the Sunday Spirit of the world of unbelief of the town in the innovation we were making.

Had dinner which was served and ate in the Community Spirit at one-half past three. About 20 minutes past four began washing, worked two and a half hours with a good degree of satisfaction at that and saw it all done, then went to my room and lay down to rest three quarters of an hour. Then attended Evening Meeting. Logs, etc. read. Some advice to Mr. Higgins and conversation till 9, then had supper of coffee, pie, cheese, etc. A treat to all and a means of Community fellowship.

Then wrote a letter to Mr. Cragin and retired about half past ten, with feelings of gratitude and a desire for fruitfulness of heart and life to God and a wish to grow in communion with Christ and loving fellowship with the church.

Two days later, the Log for March 13 records:

As to the night, felt the need of rest and was quite free from cramp. Arose at first bell, dressed and prepared for breakfast. Read some, ate breakfast, felt rather languid and depressed. Did not guess very well in Bible Game. Felt thankful and a desire to be grateful and make returns to God for his goodness, yet felt some obstructions and seemed to have to labor in spirit to see the bright, the cheerful, and hopeful sides of things, and the joy, justification and genial social Community fellowship. Resisted the spirit as an evil influence and got some victory over it and enjoyed helping Mrs. Bradley a while in getting dinner. The piece on provoking to love seemed very appropriate and I was glad to endorse and accept the spirit of it; thought it was an art that could be studied and practiced to the advantage of increased union and spiritual communion with God and with one another.

A short time after dishes were washed, the one o'clock Braiding Bee began. Enjoyed it as a social season and a good time to study and become acquainted with each others' spirits—became interested in the book Horace reads.

At one-half past two went to wood Bee till one-quarter past 4; then wrote my log for the previous day and this evening's reading. I was nearly all day haunted with the impression that I ought to write a letter to my Brother Leander and also to my brother-in-law Bliss in obedience to a sort of promise I made him to let him know something about Mr. Rounday's mill, as he wants to purchase something this spring—but how to perform I found not, but satisfied myself by promising that I would take time and write tomorrow. I can see in such experience the effect of double-mindedness—feeling of conscience about doing something and yet feeling impelled by circumstances or necessity to neglect doing it. It seems to have the same affect upon the spirit that overtasking the body or excessive labor of the hands has on the physical system. Resolved by grace to steer clear of such extremities and unfruitful positions and be single-eyed to one thing or the other.

Supper, class and meeting occupied the time till 9:00. The Oneida and other logs, etc. were quite entertaining and edifying. Mr. Waters read my log and was bothered so little to read it that I felt new courage to try to write better and make improvement, and I see that it will be effected by attention, care and patient plodding. I will confess these elements in me and union with Christ my ability to practice them.

In relation to my promise to myself to write the letter that was on my mind, I can say that I have began it.

In view of all these good resolutions, it may be that the next following logs were written but have been lost. The only remaining one is dated March 28, 1855:

Awoke quite early this morning and was occupied at first with various thoughts. Soon, however, I involuntarily thought of the past, of my youth and of youthful associations, among others, my deceased sister came to my mind. I thought with some interest on my relations to her as companion in the family relation, and our religious faith and first experiences. I wondered soon as to our present affinities and what were the present facilities of communication between us.

Next, Mrs. Langstaff's suggestion made to me the eve before met with more or less reflection. She seemed to choose a private occasion to relieve herself of the pressure of my criticism by placing at my door a sort of counter-criticism. I had criticized her for tendencies to envy and jealous feeling toward persons, and she came in a very *friendly* way to invite me to consider whether I was not partial to Sarah. I felt genial towards her admonitions and wished for the truth, but the more I reflected, the more it seemed that it was difficult for her to accept of my view and judgment of her, and that her love and attachment for me had in it the spirit of ownership and appropriation, and that the exercise of this motherly patronizing spirit was an attempt to maintain her own views and position after all. I felt conscious of some aim and motive in her that obstructed love and something in her spirit that I could not fellowship. Next, the bell rang and I arose, felt bouyant in spirit, determining to free myself of this only *little* entanglement which I realized and at last be above it in faith and hope and so met the duties of the day.

Had breakfast, Bible Game, guessed with a degree of satisfaction to myself. Next several business consultations, two calls at the door. Mr. Th— wished and got the key to the barn. Charles Knight called to obtain Bob for a chore. Despatching them, I got away to feed the pigs. It was then 8 o'clock. Next, shaved and 20 minutes past 8 went to town clerk's office, examined records of Deeds, returned at 9. Then Mrs. Noyes went to Mr. Tufts, loaned of him $25, in addition to $25 the other day. Returned to Mrs. Campbell's. Liked her better than for some time past. With Mrs. N. arrived home at 11 and one-half—went to P. Knight's home to dinner at 12. Bean porridge much enjoyed for dinner. After dinner fed the hogs, got ready and at one went to Perry Knight's, then to the Depot. Took passage on freight train for Brattleboro. Called at Mr. Mead's office, did some business with him. Had pleasant visit with Mrs. Mead and Joanna. Went into street, purchased some varnish for waggon and some leather for a pair of shoes. Walked to R.R. Depot, waited there half an hour for train.

While waiting observed the ways of persons about. Was particularly struck with the inordinate appetite of one boy for candy. He continued to buy and eat two or three sticks at a time until he had ate more than a dozen. He would eat the sticks of candy as a calf would eat ears of corn, and the boy that sold them said he had bought 20 cents worth and ate all but 3 or 4. Other boys were noticing and encouraging him by their wonderments and eccentricities. I could see much contrast in them to our children, with the fear of God and chastening discipline, and could see how the spirit of the world, the flesh and the Devil operate to brutalize and destroy.

Came home at 5. Supper of rice griddle cakes, etc.

THE CRYSTAL PALACE

HOW AND BY WHAT line of reasoning John Humphrey Noyes managed to convince himself and his Community brethren, at a time of extreme financial stringency, that he should journey to London and Paris was explained neither in the *Free Church Circular* nor in any private documents I have been able to search. There are, however, certain straws in the wind which are suggestive.

In the *Free Church Circular* for March 13, 1851, an editorial, merely signed "S," expatiates on "The World's Fair at London, giving particulars gathered from notices that have appeared in the papers of the last year in relation to the great Industrial Exhibition which is to take place in London the ensuing summer." It was to be regarded as "England's invitation or challenge to the whole world to compete with her manufacturers and mechanics in the products of their industry and taste." Suitable buildings were to be constructed and an Executive Committee on the Industrial Exhibition was appointed in the United States: "The U.S. Frigate St. Lawrence was fitted up to convey American products to the Fair and sailed from New York on the first of February. Many vessels of different nations have doubtless been freighted with the products for which these nations are respectively distinguished. 'Chinese, Turks, French, English and Americans,' says an editor who intends visiting the Fair, 'will there vie with each other for the prize to be awarded superior skill. This assembly of the nations must greatly tend to destroy national pride, ignorance and prejudice, the great sources of war. The exhibition was to be opened on the first of May and to continue six months."

A month later, in the issue of the *Free Church Circular* for April 16, 1851, came the second straw in the wind: "Our family had an excellent entertainment a few evenings since, in the reading of 'The Private History of the Glass Palace,' and in conversing about the Industrial Fair. Wishing to have our readers sympathize with us in our interest in this first World's Convention, we have been induced to publish the article"—which they did, at length. It was entitled *Private History of the Palace of Glass* (from Dickens).

Considering that Mr. Noyes, their leader and the director of all their enthusiasms, was due to sail for England to visit this same Exhibition on April 16, the day of publication of that number of the *Circular*, it can be imagined with what interest the little commune family "conversed" about the Industrial Fair. Perhaps it might also have been said that Mr. N., "wishing to have the members of his flock sympathize with *his* interest" in the subject, had been the voice which induced them to publish the article.

This, of course, is mere speculation. The only direct mention of John Humphrey Noyes in this issue is a brief note stating that he and Mr. R. S. DeLatre would leave New York that day on the steamer *Baltic* for England. DeLatre, English born, was an enthusiastic convert to Oneida communism who had tried to form a similar group in Canada. His attempt failed and he joined the Oneida commune five years later. On April 25, Mr. Miller contributed a note to the paper giving notice of the setting forth of their travellers: "I had the pleasure of seeing our friends J. H. Noyes and R. S. DeLatre on board the *Baltic* on Wednesday last; and though there was a severe storm at the time, they left in fine spirits. The storm raged furiously all that afternoon and night, yet we had no unpleasant feelings in thinking of them, for we were sure the He who commands the winds and waves would protect them. And now, by a beautiful providence, He has let us know that they have safely weathered the terrific gale. We learn by the *Tribune* that the *Pacific*, which arrived in New York on Saturday, passed the *Baltic* at three o'clock on Friday last, thirty-nine hours after she sailed, 310 miles from New York."

They had still heard nothing from the travellers, but on May 22, the *Tribune* announced the safe arrival of the *Baltic* in Liverpool, together with what they rightly call "a harrowing account by Mr. Greeley" of the *seasickness* on board, which was scarcely mitigated by the extra accommodations and attentions that the sumptuous steamship afforded. "Of every hundred who cross the Atlantic," he wrote, "I am confident that two-thirds endure more than they would do during two months hard labor as convicts in State Prison."

This would seem to make it clear that the item which spoke of "an editor who intended to visit the Fair" referred to Horace Greeley of the *New York Tribune*, of whom John Humphrey Noyes has much to say in his account of the ocean crossing which he learned to enjoy and which Mr. Greeley did not.

In the same issue of the *Free Church Circular*, April 16, 1851, Mr. Noyes, in an article on Business Principles, written from Brooklyn on March 1, discusses "a very common method of cheating ourselves and another." He gives as example a little boy who "expressed a desire to go to bed, got the little lamp and lighted it with much satisfaction, but then did not want to go to bed, thus proving that his real intention was only to *light the lamp*—the purpose which will hold and bind him. Whatever it is which he professes to make his real purpose, if it does not charm him it will not bind him."

There is no way of proving what is no more than a conjecture, but it seems at least a possible guess that "that which charmed" John Noyes might have been the tempting opportunity to spread to the world the news of his new-minted religion and its fruits in communal living.

Merely to see the famous Crystal Palace or the other exhibits of the Industrial Fair would seem too frivolous and objective to justify the expense at this time. It is possible that he had an ambition to proselytize in England and perhaps France. England was the home of Robert Owen and France the home of Charles Fourier, both of whom had exported socialistic ideas from their mother countries to the new world. Whether Noyes hoped to reverse this proceeding cannot be known.

Another possible guess is that he took Robert DeLatre with him as a native sponsor who would introduce him in the right quarters. Their immediate visit to "Mr. A——" in Liverpool suggests such a thing, rather than that "Mr. A——" was already a Noyes partisan, since Noyes writes, "Mr. A——'s religious sentiments are high churchism *plus* Irvingism, a singular mixture of formalism with fanaticism." However it was during this visit, that host and guest quarrelled over the translation of a Greek word, an argument which Noyes won with the comment, "This is a specimen of our debates with him and two of his brother clergymen." The Americans finally left, presenting their hosts with two *Bereans*, two *Confessions*, and a *Faith-fact* tract. "So much for our spiritual labors."

In his first letter home, Mr. Noyes, writing from Liverpool on April 29, 1851, observed first "that the road to England is *hilly*. The *Baltic* is a big ship, but the waves of the ocean are bigger and I found that the idea of our riding over them like ripples was only a pleasant illusion. In fact, the big ship tossed about all the way very much as the yawl of the sloop is tossed when the wind blows fresh in the bay. The wind was against us nearly all the time and frequently in our teeth.

"Now I must tell you how I got along as to seasickness, etc. I was in a deadly clinch with the demon of the sea, as I expected, within two hours from the start. Through that whole afternoon and night we pitched and rolled in the midst of a roaring confusion of winds and waters. Well, I met the enemy in this case precisely as I met the Cholera. The temptation to sea-sickness and especially to fear, was tremendous. Sickness prevailed throughout the ship. Mr. DeLatre took to his berth and I had no benefit of his society for several days. My mind was very busy with faith and philosophy, and worked well. I kept about, frequently on deck, training myself to take pleasure in the motion. My appetite at supper the first day was not good, but I mumbled and swallowed a piece of bread. I slept but little that night but a blessed victory was worked out in my spirit and the next day I was as well as usual. I lost not a meal afterwards and came virtually to enjoy the scallops and varied curves as the ship danced over the deep."

The next letter, dated May 11, 1851, gives us our only direct clue to the purpose of the expedition. "We have found an unexpected and admirable opening for the exhibition of *our* contributions to the great Fair. By a curious and beautiful process of providence we have been introduced to C—— and D——, the socialist writers, and have been very favorably received by them. We have presented both of them a copy of the *Berean* and the *Reports* and *Religious History*. D—— was much interested in our exposé, and made us welcome to the freest intercourse with him while we stay here, and is to give us letters of introduction to his brother and others in Paris. I shall call on him on Wednesday, and if he is not by that time staggered by his reading of our books, I think we shall secure him as a friend, if not as a brother. We could not find a better point of connection with the progressives of both England and France. So, you see *I have exhibited my invention* as I said I would" (emphasis added).

What exactly, beyond the distribution of Oneida Community literature, he meant by "our contribution" and "my invention" there is no way of learning. The rest of his correspondence with his wife is taken up with descriptions of sight-seeing. An amusing episode which he related took place at the Crystal Palace. Oddly enough, this Yankee egalitarian "had quite a desire to see the Queen, was unwilling to go back without being able to say I had seen Her Majesty." On their last day they revisited the Crystal Palace, Mr. Noyes "determined to enter into the glories of the scene with the abandonment of inspiration." Presently he stopped with a group of people "who seemed especially interested in some sight." He took his place by a railing and saw beyond it

> a group of ordinary-looking folks examining the articles of the show, among them a plain sort of matron leaning on a gentleman's arm. I asked a bystander of very distinguished air who that lady might be. "My dear sir," said he, "It is the Queen." There was I, with my republican hat on, face to face with Her Majesty, not ten yards distant. The latent loyalty of the old Norfolk blood awoke and I respectfully uncovered. "And who is that tall gentleman with the Queen?" I said to him of the distinguished air. "That," said he, "is the Prince of Prussia." I had an opportunity to inspect the royal countenance at my leisure for some minutes without crowding or bustle. The Queen is not beautiful—the portraits flatter her. She appears simple and sensible. Her stature is short and her features rather coarse. But there is something good and even majestic in her eye. Her dress was quite ordinary. After some minutes she, with her suite, came directly towards the railing at the point where I was, passing me within reach of my hand, with her face toward me and bowing two or three times as she swept along to another stall.

The day before Noyes left London a notice of the Oneida Association appeared in the New York correspondence in the *London Daily News*:

> A fanatical association existing in Oneida County in this state has published a report of its progress for the last year. It con-

sists of one or two hundred men and about 60 women. These are the indiscriminate associates of the men. But two or three children have been born in the Association for the last year. It claims a large degree of prosperity from its cultivation of the soil, and its religious code is based entirely on a new theory of the communication with the spirits of the other world. It is avowed as a part of their belief that the spirits have advanced so far towards an intimacy with the human race that they are beginning to have power to form intimacies in consequence of which marriage, according to human and divine law, must now of necessity be abrogated. You may imagine to what a pass things are coming among these new lights. And yet what I relate in this letter is not generally known here. I would not have believed what I write you if I had not seen the report in question.

John Humphrey Noyes made reply:

To the Editor of the *Daily News*. Sir: Trusting that you prefer correct information to crudities and errors, even in a matter of small consequence, I notify you that your American correspondent, in his hasty attempt to give an idea of the Association established at Oneida County, New York, misleads you in several particulars. I have been identified with that Association from its beginning; and can speak as one familiar with its history and principles. Instead of its "religious code being based entirely on the new theory or communication with the spirits of the other world" as your correspondent asserts, its faith was established and published 16 years ago, long before the "rappings" were heard of; and the central article of its belief, on which its whole religious code is based, is that *Christ is a savior from sin in this world*. It has no connection whatever with the "rappings," having never been visited by these phenomena. The allusion to them in its last *Report* was quite incidental; not indicating, as your correspondent supposes, the fundamental idea of the Association. The statement also that the Association "consists of one or two hundred men and about 60 women" is quite incorrect. The *Report* from which your correspondent professes to derive his information, is the statement of the number of members as follows:

Number of adult members (males 69, females 66)   135
Youth and children (males 36, females 34)   70

Whole number of members (males 105, females 100)   205

If it is true as your correspondent affirms, that the history and principles of the Oneida Association 'are not generally known' in America, it is not our fault. We have published *three* successive

Annual Reports and several books and pamphlets. We publish also a weekly paper. If you have any curiosity to know more about us, and will address me at Brooklyn, New York, or send me your paper containing this correction, I will forward to you the document which will enable you to give full and true information about the new and alarming development of socialism which your correspondent has discovered in America.

Respectfully yours,

John H. Noyes.

Shortly after his return, John Humphrey Noyes in a Home Talk carried in the *Free Church Circular* for June 20, 1851, passed on the fruits of wisdom he had gathered in his journey:

One of the practical lessons I learned and one of the most serious impressions I received was that most Americans are making a great mistake in undertaking too much, under the idea of traveling in Europe. I believe there are a great many Americans who might go and see the wonders of London and even a few days in Paris, who, if they then could come home would make a good trip of it but who are utterly unfit to go further—to travel Europe, as it is called. They do not understand the languages—they are cheated at every turn and find they are every way out of their depth. They get heartily sick of it and would be glad to go home, but they are committed; they have paid for their passage across the ocean and are too proud not to get their money's worth. They are afraid their friends would laugh at them if they should go back without seeing all there is to be seen.

I will mention two or three things in the way of preparation for the voyage that I learned by feeling the need of them. I should in the first place carry a *map* of the ocean and the countries I was to visit. I could find but one map on board the *Baltic* and none on the *Asia*. My advice in respect to other things would be exactly the opposite of Mr. Greeley's. In regard to feet, he advises people to get a thick pair of cowhide boots, put them on at the beginning of the voyage and stick to them till the end of it. If I were going again, one of the first things I should do would be to provide myself with light shoes or slippers—as light and comfortable as possible, to walk in on board ship and on land. If the business is to be travelling and sight-seeing, the preparation of the feet is a matter of a good deal of importance.

Mr. Greeley said the first day that he expected to be sick through the whole voyage. I told him if that was his calculation, he would undoubtedly be sick: and according to his faith it was done unto him. One chief cause of sea-sickness is a conflict between your heart and your circumstances. You are accustomed to living on a firm foundation, on ground and floors that are immoveable—accustomed to moving about in straight lines instead of galloping. But here your house is on horseback, you have to eat, drink, sleep etc., with your house galloping under you. The mind and imagination and will don't like it; it produces the same sensation as homesickness. The meaning of it is that the will is at war with circumstances. It is simply a case of very virulent *discontent.* The same trust in God that looks to him in all vicissitudes, the same faith that makes you flexible and submissive to your circumstances, here will save you from sea-sickness.

I had more of a fight with fear than I had with sea-sickness; but I conquered it by an extension of the same principle that I applied to sea-sickness. I found it was accompanied by a wish that we might not have any more storms. But I made up my mind as to what weather we were likely to have, and expected it, and submitted to it in advance. Resistance to the motion of the vessel produces a sensation just as though the soul and body were parting. The body must go down with the ship in all its rollings and surgings, but the soul, choosing its accustomed equilibrium, refuses to go and hence a feeling of discord is produced.

DISASTROUS EVENTS

T HE YEARS 1850-1852 were made memorable for the Oneida
Community by several disastrous events. That they weathered
them all and, in fact, did not even mention the first in the
Free Church Circular for 1850, is characteristic of their determined
optimism and faith in Providence. This first event was not unexpected by men and women who had lived through the attack
and exodus from Putney but it was a painful ordeal and, as it
happened, an illegal one.

It is our misfortune that, so far as I have been able to discover in what remains of the archives, all documents relating to
the encounter between the Oneida Community and the law, in
either Madison or Oneida County, have been destroyed. It seems
obvious that such documents must have existed and that they
must have been extant in 1934 or 1935 when Robert Allerton
Parker visited Kenwood and was given access to the O C Archives,
then in the keeping of George W. Noyes. If this assumption is correct, then the chapter in Parker's book, *A Yankee Saint* (p. 187-89)
is based on those now missing reports.

The only other history of the Community which refers to
this affair is *Oneida: Utopian Community to Modern Corporation*,
by Maren Lockwood Carden (pp. 80-81). Written a generation
after Parker's and twenty years after the destruction of the archives, this work evidently depends for its facts on Parker's
statements, although it contains one or two unimportant mistakes.
Mrs. Carden says, first, that "the residents of Madison and of the
adjacent Oneida County brought independent suits against the

Community." No suits were ever actually brought. She also suggests that "the Perfectionists' apparent prosperity . . . had won them a few friends in the neighborhood." That the Perfectionists actually had won friends is perfectly true, but it strains the credulity to believe that this was attributable to their "apparent prosperity" at a time when they were working like Trojans and living often on two meals a day.

Parker writes: "wild tales concerning Noyes and his followers aroused increasing scandal and gossip." It is not to be wondered at that the Communists, especially those who remembered Putney—"the persecution, the threats of mob violence, the final expulsion from Vermont"—felt apprehensive.

> In 1850, enemies complained to magistrates of both Oneida and Madison Counties concerning the 'unmoralities' practiced within the Community. The question was referred to the Grand Jury of Madison County. Information was given and complaint made by certain persons residing in the town of Lenox that there was in their midst a collection of individuals of both sexes, living in a mixed manner, that they did not hold to marriage; that their numbers were steadily on the increase; that their example was corrupting and demoralizing to the community in which they lived and that, in fact, they were a public nuisance. The Grand Jury was asked to find a bill of indictment against them. A number of witnesses backed this complaint. Many questions were asked of the complainants and witnesses, from which it appeared that such a collection of people did live in the county. But it also became evident that they were industrious, peaceable and law-abiding, apparently minding their own business and harming no one, not differing from other people essentially except as to their views on marriage. A number of Jurors were for finding against Noyes and his followers. Finally the Grand Jury tactfully decided not to notice the complaint, but to keep an eye on the behavior and influence of the Communists.

It is to be supposed that the men and women at Oneida breathed a sigh of relief at this deliverance, but their reprieve was premature. According to Parker, while the legal forces in Utica, Oneida County, knew nothing of the confrontation in neighboring Madison County, they evidently heard rumors too, and decided to attack on their own account. This was the more outrageous since the Community's legal residence was not in Oneida County and therefore the Oneida County authorities had no jurisdiction over them. Nevertheless, they summoned a number of men and women of the Community to appear before their Grand Jury and in Utica, as Parker writes, "put them through a merciless examination by an exasperated District Attorney before a very chilly Grand Jury. It was not fair nor lawful that they should be called on to incriminate themselves, but they were; and they told the truth and the whole truth. Parker writes:

> Sensitive and high-minded women were asked obscene questions about their most private experiences; but without evasion or complaint they told all. The women were never to forget the ignominy of this ordeal. They ran the gauntlet of the curious gaze of idlers, the leers, the suppressed obscenities, the quips of lesser functionaries, the malicious probing of lecherous lawyers and dignitaries. But their dignity, their perfect manners and their honesty carried them through. They were fully conscious that they were in the lion's mouth. How they ever got out they never quite discovered. All they could ever recall was that they had told the furious District Attorney and the excited newspaper world that they were willing to go back to marriage or Shakerism if that were demanded of them. Their inquisitors answered with scorn and wrath; they had no confidence in John Noyes. They advised his followers to break up and "clear out." The women answered meekly that they had no idea of resisting the will of the magistracy and people around them; that if it was really the will of neighbors that they should clear out, they would do so.

The Community's only reference to this affair is given as the last answer to a series of questions "most frequently asked by strangers" published in 1851. The Question, #36, was: "Do you expect to be tolerated by the world around you?".

The Answer:

> The prospect is fair in this respect. We were abused in Vermont, but have been well treated in New York. Several temporary excitements have been stirred up against us in the circle of our immediate neighbors by the efforts of deserters; and by firebrands that have pursued us from Vermont. But they have always soon subsided, without serious hostilities. We have recently had a trial of this kind, owing partly to imprudence of our own, which, however, has terminated amicably. It threatened for a time to bring us into collision

with the State Authorities; but finally proved to be only an occasion of testing and manifesting their liberality. It also led to an open expression of the feelings of our neighbors, which we think goes far toward settling the question of toleration in our favor. We have always stood ready, in New York as in Vermont, to leave our settlement peaceably, and seek other quarters, if the people around us should pronounce us a nuisance; and in order to ascertain the state of our neighbors' feelings, we recently circulated among them a document of which the following is a copy.

To the District Attorney of the County of Oneida, and All Whom It May Concern: —

This is to certify that we, the undersigned, citizens of the towns of Vernon and Lenox, are well acquainted with the general character of the Oneida Community, and are willing to testify that we regard them as honorable business men, as good neighbors, and quiet peaceable citizens. We believe them to be lovers of justice and good order—that they are men who mind their own business, and in no way interfere with the rights of their neighbors. We regard them, so far as we know, as persons of good moral character; and we have no sympathy with the recent attempts to disturb their peace.

This was readily signed by nearly everyone we asked, and in most cases with hearty good will. The largest land-owner and the most influential citizen in the Oneida Reserve, voluntarily said to those who called on him as he had to others, that he considered us not only good peaceable citizens but the best class in the region; and he regarded it as a blessing to the people around, to have us in their midst.

This influential citizen was the Honorable Timothy Jenkins, Representative to Congress for the years 1844, 1846, 1850. He had also been District Attorney for Oneida County earlier, 1840-45. It would appear, since one of his successors was appointed District Attorney on April 22, 1850, for one year, that the "exasperated" and "furious" District Attorney who vituperated the communists may have been the notorious Roscoe Conkling, later known to fame for a scandal in Washington which involved what the Oneida Communists would have considered "carnal behavior." If that is true, it was a nice piece of poetic justice.

However it was, it would seem that the editor of the Community *Circular*, November 30, 1851, at least, bore no malice. In an editorial on "Tolerance" he writes:

In contrast with the course pursued in Putney, Gamaliel's principle of non-intervention prevails in the State of New York. We have been well treated by the people immediately around us, though our principles are fully known and the emissaries of the Putney inquisition have done all they could to disturb our relations with our neighbors. Our first annual *Report* has met with a civil and in most cases a favorable reception in the most respectable quarters.

Another important fact which our experience goes to establish is, that of the three learned professions which rule society and determine public opinion, viz.; the doctors, the lawyers, and the priests, the lawyers are far the most liberal toward us. There is a class of pettifoggers it is true; but we have found lawyers who are really well educated and in good practice to be immeasurably superior to the doctors and priests in the civilization of free thought and discussion.

This may have been a thank-offering to the Hon. Timothy Jenkins who championed them in their hour of need. And if the reference to a "pettifogger" was a covert gibe at the less honorable Roscoe Conkling, perhaps the Communists should be forgiven for being only human.

The second calamity was less of an ordeal, except financially. An *Extra*, appearing as a final issue of the *Free Church Circular*, Oneida Reserve, July 15, 1851, reported the event:

We take the first convenient opportunity to inform our subscribers of the suspension (for the present) of our printing operations, including the *Circular*, and the reason why. The building which was used for our printing office, store, shoe-shop, sterotype-foundry, etc., was destroyed by fire on Saturday evening, July 5, and with it both presses, a large share of the type, and all publications on hand, with the exception of the *Bereans*. For facilities to make the present communication we are indebted to the politeness of Mr. Howlett of the *Central NY Journal* office, Vernon. As our readers may have a natural desire to know the particulars of this occurrence, we will not omit to give a brief sketch.

On the evening above mentioned, the Association were all, as usual, in general assembly. It was about nine o'clock—we had been talking about individual inspiration and had just passed a resolution that we would every one rely on interior direction for guidance of our conduct for the coming week. The subject was concluded and the conversation rested; a member requested to have the 13th chapter of Romans read and the Bible was just opened when we suddenly started to our feet by an indefinite alarm. Upon the first rush forward, someone said, "quiet!"—Moderation was restored and the egress from the room was free and still.

There was a simultaneous gush of gratitude from all hearts when it appeared that it was only the store that was in peril, not our home buildings. A proud column of flame was already issuing from the roof, which defied all the resistance that could be made without an engine. An attempt was made, however, and for a few minutes the virtue of all the water that could be brought was vigorously applied. It was vain; the rescue was soon abandoned and all turned their exertions to removing the contents of the doomed structure.

The fire took in the garret, from some unknown cause. Our printing office was on the second floor and was invaded by the destroyer before its doors were opened. A large hole was burned through the plastering just over the power press. The progress of the fire was rapid but orderly and graceful—sweeping clean in its descent from the roof to the foundation. There was helpfulness and energy on all sides, without distracting excitement. Everything in the store and shoe-shop was got out and carried to a place of safety before the light of the fire was dim on our walks. In less than three hours we were reassembled, with the exception of a few sentinels, in the room we had left, congratulating each other on the general good luck, and inquiring for God's meaning. The event has afforded us many profitable reflections, but it suffices for the present to say that we take it as "conservative fire"; and are sure of profiting by this criticism of God's providence. Those of our friends who are acquainted with our history will not be disturbed by an irregularity in the publication of our paper, which is something which is well known we have never been over-scrupulous to avoid. If they reason as we do, they will assuredly anticipate a resurrection from the ashes of this fire in an auspicious time, not very distant and happily in a new and improved form.

The pecuniary loss by this fire is probably about $3,000.00.

The next publication by the Association bore a dateline of Brooklyn, N.Y., and a date of November 6, 1851. It was in a different and much larger format than the previous magazine and its title had been changed to simply *The Circular*. "Published weekly, Devoted to the Sovereignty of Jesus Christ. Editor, J. H. Noyes." The leading editorial explained the change as:

really a continuation of the *Free Church Circular* (editors G. W. Noyes & H. H. Skinner) published until recently at Oneida; the *Spiritual Magazine, Perfectionist,* and the *Witness* published through a succession of years at Putney, Vt.; and the *Perfectionist,* published in 1834 at New Haven, Connecticut. Readers who are acquainted with those periodicals will need no *programme* of our principles; and others may as well be left to find us out by trying us.

The editor simply begs leave to observe by way of personal introduction, that he returns to his post, after an interval of five years devoted to labors in the details of practical association, with a consciousness of improved qualifications, and with fresh attraction and devotion to his old calling.

The fire which destroyed the printing office and press at Oneida, and thus abruptly terminated the *Free Church Circular,* spared the greater part of our type—sufficient for the use of this paper—and made occasion for the transfer of the printing department to Brooklyn. We have since built a printing office in the rear of our building, procured a power press, and made all arrangements necessary for efficient and permanent service in the work before us. Our working company of writers, reporters and printers is stronger than ever before and ready as one man for any amount of service that the times may demand.

Since Noyes, the new editor, was a practical man as well as a theorist, he finished this greeting with a frank statement of the financial needs of the new publication and an earnest request for contributions from "those who wish to enlist with us as reliable supporters of this press." Experience had shown that ordinary subscriptions could not be relied on for support. He proposed instead that every enthusiast for the cause agree to remit a dollar or more once a month for the support of the paper. It was an excellent piece of promotional writing but it may be said now that it did not then or ever bring in anything like enough to support the enterprise. Actually, at the end of his publishing career, in 1879, Noyes explained in closing the last issue of the *American Socialist* that the Oneida Community had, in the course of its publishing life, spent at least $100,000 of its own money to underwrite its press. At that point, with the Community itself on the verge of dissolution, he was finally obliged to abandon his lifelong infatuation with the press.

During the first two months of the new *Circular,* the editor printed two statements of the relationship of the two communes. The first appeared on November 15, 1851:

Brooklyn and Oneida. The Brooklyn company which is engaged in the business of this paper, has heretofore been *called* sometimes a *branch* of the Oneida Association. Strictly speaking, however, it is an independent company; and so far as there is affiliation between the two, the Oneida Association is the branch. The relations of the editor of this paper to the Oneida Association are simply these: 1. He was prominently active in the original organization of that community, and the first contributor to its funds. 2. He labored with and for that Community in all sorts of service—from laying stone wall to preaching—during the first years of its existance. 3. He has since been in active and constant correspondence and frequent personal communication with the members of that Community. But, fourthly, he has visited that Community but twice since February 1849, and not at all for more than two years past. He has done and will do what he can, consistently with other duties, for the good management and success of that Community, and he hopes and expects to see it emerge from all its tribulations, unblamable and prosperous; but he assumes no such care over it or responsibility for it, as would exclude the sovereignty of God or the responsibility of its members.

This would seem a curious kind of washing of hands by the man who had certainly inspired and founded the Oneida Community which was, at the time of writing, actually supporting the Brooklyn branch, whether or not he wished to acknowledge it. Perhaps this thought occurred to him later, for in the issue of December 2, he reprinted this statement, all but the final sentence, and substituted a description of the Brooklyn station:

The Brooklyn Station was commenced by a detachment from Oneida, in the spring of 1849. We occupied but one house the first two years. Last Spring we bought an adjoining house—an exact mate of the first—and converted the two into one by cutting doors through the partition wall. The basement of one house, by new arrangements, makes a spacious kitchen with cellars etc., attached, while the whole length of the other basement is converted into a diningroom. By taking away the fence which separated the backyards of the two houses, we enlarged our out-door liberties and at the same time gained room for our printing office. The establishment now accommodates a family of about thirty members. The editing, printing and mailing of this paper is a part of the family business.

In the issue for January 4, 1852, they headed the editorial column with an article on "A Family Press":

> We have been interested in the fact that while the *Circular* is offered freely to the public, so there is no paid labor in its production; from the editor without a salary, to the little hands that claim a share in the last manipulations of folding it for the mail, it goes forth from the bosom of a family who find their happiness and reward in the service. The Editor's Sanctum is in the most sociable corner of the sitting room; a pencil and bookcover serve as an *escritoir*. The compositors' work is "up stairs" and is reckoned in the programme of family arrangements as much as the cooking. Two or three have regular work there, but all our women and the children not too young are learning; and alternate between the different departments of domestic care and setting type. And they count the last as the cream of their work. In this way more than twenty have a share in getting out the paper. The press-room is in the backyard, but a step from the hall door—a building erected for the purpose. Convenient to this is the door of our diningroom where there is a long stationary table; and here it is that we fold the *Circular* of a Saturday afternoon for the mail. So we serve our reader from the dinner board which God spreads for us day by day. Much pains have been taken to make this room a place of worship and elevated associations, we consider this, among others, a consecrating ordinance.

It is perhaps ironic that this new "place of worship and elevated association" should be in a house formerly owned by Abram Smith. To that house first came the news of the death of Mary Cragin.

Of Abram Smith the *Report* merely says that he was "an old associate in the cause of holiness" who had bought the Brooklyn house at a cost of $3300 and, when he joined the Oneida Association in the spring of 1849, presented them with this building as a residence. No mention is made in the *Report* of his having been practically excommunicated after the affair with the Cragins in 1840 or that he was readmitted, after signing a very repentant confession in 1849. At this time he sold to the Community the sloop *Rebecca Ford*. He finally seceded in 1857.

The destruction of the printing office at Oneida by fire occurred on July 5, 1851. Three weeks later, on July 25, came the most tragic disaster of all. The first intelligence of this event

reached Mr. Noyes at Brooklyn in a telegram from Henry Burnham, from Poughkeepsie: "Serious news to communicate. At six
minutes past one o'clock this afternoon in a squall of about two
minutes duration, the sloop capsized and sunk. The women went
down with her, the men were saved. She was homeward bound
one mile above Hyde Park. I shall take the seven o'clock train this
evening for Brooklyn. (signed) Your stricken brother, H. W.
Burnham."

The acquisition of the sloop was new and exciting to the
communists. During the past season of 1850 she had been regular-
ly employed in freighting limestone from Kingston on the North
River to Brooklyn and New York City. The sloop was manned by
community men who, knowing nothing of navigation, "found it
necessary at the outset to get free of the trammels of the world, to
follow inspiration and keep the spiritual foremost," which meant
seamanship of their own invention.

In the beginning they were filled with enthusiasm. "We
were all elated at the prospect which opened before us in connection with this business on the river. We agreed that it should be a
community school for studying navigation. Friday night they went
up to Kingston, loaded up and came down on Sunday, only 12
hours. They proposed to have Hial and Louisa Waters go to Kingston and live at Mr. Long's."

Whether or not this last arrangement was ever completed
we have no information. Francis Long was apparently a resident of
Rondout, Abram Smith's old home, and he was later to be the
"navigator" on duty when the sloop capsized. His letter to the
local paper after the tragedy suggests that he was a recent convert
but perhaps not a satisfactory one, since it was later stated that
Mary Cragin's presence on board the sloop on that fatal voyage
was for the purpose of bringing Mr. Long into a better spirit. He
gave no testimony as to whether or not her efforts had succeeded.
Our only other information about him is that he formally joined
the Oneida Community with his family on April 19, 1851, and
seceded with them on September 22 of that year.

The first newspaper account of the disaster appeared in the
New York Tribune on July 28.

> *Sloop sunk and two women drown.* The sloop, *Rebecca
> Ford*, owned and manned by the Oneida Community, was capsized

and sunk on Saturday P.M. on the North River, while on her way to
this city, loaded with limestone. Six persons, viz., Captain A. C.
Smith, Henry W. Burnham, Francis Long, Henry J. Seymour, Mrs.
Mary E. Cragin and Miss Eliza A. Allen were on board. The women
and three of the men (Messers Smith, Burnham and Seymour) were
at dinner in the cabin when a very violent squall struck the vessel.
Perceiving a commotion but not apprehending any serious danger,
the men went on deck. The vessel immediately careened, so as to
shift her load, came on her beam ends, filled by the hatches and
cabin windows, and went down in forty feet of water. The women,
who had remained in the cabin, were lost. The men, by swimming
and by help of articles from the wreck, kept themselves afloat till
they were picked up by Captain Hotaling of the schooner *Shaw
Abbilena*, who went to them in his yawl with noble promptitude,
and afterwards generously placed his vessel at their service. Mr. Burnham had looked at his watch while at the table and noticed that it
was about five minutes past one. His watch was stopped by the
water at just six minutes past one. Two hours before the accident,
Mrs. Cragin was reading aloud to a part of the crew the 8th Chapter
of Romans and directing attention with much vivacity to the last
verse.

The *Rondout Courier* gave much the same account of the
disaster but took the occasion to enlighten their readers as to the
community. It had been located, they said, at South Rondout
some years ago and had existed also at Wilbur, New York, but had
since removed, or was about to remove once more to South Rondout. They wrote further that the community of 1840 was essentially the same as that of 1851 and that Abram C. Smith, the mas-
ter of the *Rebecca Ford*, was the head and front of the institution.
It existed on the principle of common stock and joint labor, which
was not objectionable, but it went further and extended its doctrine to a community of wives in which "all the vicious inclina-
tions of corrupt man have full sway." Until this accident the editor
had believed that by "the dispersion of the cage of unclean birds
in 1840, they had been scattered, never to pollute our shores again.
But the dog will return to his vomit and the swine to the mire."

To this attack Mr. Long, the unhappy helmsman who was
held responsible for the loss of the vessel, bravely came forward to
reply in the *Circular*, November 16, 1851. He offered a statement
of facts, prepared by J. H. Noyes who

is and has been the head of the Community since its commencement.

1. There is no branch or member of the Oneida Community residing at Rondout, and no establishment of the kind is contemplated.

2. There has never been a branch of that Community at Rondout. Abram Smith, who is now connected with that Community, has resided at Rondout since 1837 till about two years ago. But he never formed a Community there and lived peaceably with his family in the usual way, with the exception of a short period of irregularity about the year 1840, till the death of his wife. He was not connected with the Oneida Community at the time of that irregularity, but on the contrary, was excommunicated from the fellowship of those who have since formed the Oneida Community and remained excluded till after the death of his wife in 1849. His general character is known at Rondout and must speak for itself. The Oneida Community is responsible for his proceedings only since the death of his wife.

3. The branch of the Community that owned the *Rebecca Ford* resides at Brooklyn, near New York.

4. The main Association resides at Oneida Reserve, near Oneida Depot, N.Y., where its behavior has secured not only toleration but respect from the community around.

5. The Association has published three annual *Reports* in which its principles and practices are fully and frankly avowed. These should be referred to instead of lying reports, by those who wish to know and circulate truth.

To this statement Mr. Long added handsomely a personal word: "As far as blame is to be attached to individuals in this case, a good share must fall on me; as I stood at the helm at the time of the accident and failed to foresee and call the counsel and assistance from those who were more experienced than myself." As to the charges against the Oneida Community, he said firmly that the advice he had received from the leading members of the Association had led him to a just appreciation of moral purity.

What happened immediately after receiving word of the accident was recounted in a letter from John Humphrey Noyes to Mr. Cragin three days later. He had gone directly to Kingston where he left Mr. Long to keep a warning light on the sloop's mast which projected some three feet above water at low tide. After holding a sort of inquest he, with Mr. Seymour and Abram Smith, unanimously concluded that Long's misjudgment and cowardice were the direct cause of the disaster. "That the perverse spirit in him which has resisted criticism and kindness so long was the previous chronic cause; and that the loose habits of fellowship which have admitted him among us and employed him in responsible business have involved the Association in his culpability; so that this chastisement is deserving and necessary for us all. Mr. Long had been for months in a gloomy, unbelieving, non-consulting spirit. One main object of Mrs. Cragin's excursion on the sloop was to make a last effort to conquer him by kindness and advice."

On November 30, 1851, the *Circular* published a detailed statement from Henry Burnham. They had left Brooklyn at 4 o'clock in the afternoon, sailed forty miles, and anchored for the night near Stony Point. The next day, after going ashore for various reasons, they passed the night two miles above Newburgh. Near Rondout they loaded the vessel and all returned on board before noon. Burnham took the helm and remained on duty until nearly one o'clock.

> The day was fine; the wind blew from the west mainly but was quite "contrary" nevertheless by close attention to the helm, mainsheet, etc., we laid our course and congratulated one another upon our speed and good luck.
>
> Dinner was ready at one, and the men were called below. Mr. Long offered to relieve me at the helm and I accepted. The wind had lulled to a quiet breeze; everything seemed to be right on deck and we sat down to our dinner with buoyant hearts. Not the least premonition of danger disturbed our spirits. We had commenced eating when we felt the effects of a sudden flaw from the west. Without any particular apprehension of danger, I stepped up to look out, which was quite natural for me.
>
> I saw it was a severe gust, and walked out, followed immediately by Captain Smith. His quick eye observed that Long was maneuvering badly at the helm, and he took his place. But it was too late; the sloop had gone over too far to right herself, and there was no getting into the cabin. I sustained myself by clinging to the guards of the starboard quarter and as she careened over, took my place on the side of the vessel which proved to be longest out of water. From the point I could see all. The stones on deck were going with a crash and everything was chaos in the cabin. Mr. Seymour was the last one that escaped from thence, and he, on reaching the deck, stepped into the water. Mr. Smith saw Miss Allen but could render her no assistance. The hatches were open and the sloop filled almost instantly.

I was self-possessed but helpless as a child. My inexperience in swimming, when finding myself afloat, made my case hopeless, unless God should interpose. And he did interpose the help of one of the oars and then a plank which floated directly to me. I buoyed myself up without any difficulty until we were picked up. We lingered about the spot while the least hope remained, and did not abandon it until after the mast disappeared. It was not until after we had gone aboard the *Abilena* while drying our clothes that the reality of our circumstances came over me. The sensation with Mr. Seymour was simultaneous; we wept like children.

The grim last offices were attended to by John Noyes who went to the scene of the wreck next day and arranged for the raising of the sloop. As stated in the *Circular*, November 6, 1851: "On the 19th of August the bodies were taken from the cabin, laid side by side in one coffin, clad, as they went down, in short dresses of the Oneida uniform, and buried with appropriate exercises in a cemetery belonging to the Episcopal Church of Esopus, whose obelisk rises on the West bank of the Hudson nearly opposite Hyde Park. A monument of white marble was erected over the grave. Beside the inscriptions which gave the life statistics of the two women were the words, 'Gilbert Johnson, a resident of Esopus, kindly gave the strangers a grave.'"

The final word for the Community was written by John Humphrey Noyes in the *Circular*, November 30, 1851:

Vitality, hope, success are pictured on the main breadth of our canvas, but here, almost at the center, is a terrible death scene. We are rising triumphant, but where are our sweetest and brightest fellow-laborers? We are rebuked in the midst of victory. *"Serve the Lord with fear, rejoice with trembling; he will not give his glory to another, nor his praise to graven images."* To exalt in success, as though *we* had achieved it, is to *embezzle* the property of the government we serve. The king of kings takes no counsel from fear of the party opposed to him, and his dealings with his own party and his own officers—they will not escape criticism under the shelter of favortism or policy.

"Judgment begins at the house of God." We have accepted this condition of service. We have invited the chastisements which we feel. Let us then remember the integrity of God and beware of embezzlement. We shall escape the rod only by ceasing to need it, and we shall invite prosperity only by being able to bear it without glorying. "All the haughtiness of man shall be brought low, and the Lord alone shall be exalted."

On February 1, 1852, the Oneida Community's paper, *The Circular*, reported, under the heading *Voice of the Press*, a verbal attack by a New York religious newspaper, *The Observer*, upon the Community and its unorthodox beliefs and behavior. *The Circular*'s tone was faintly ironic:

> The editor apparently disapproves of our principles, but he gives his readers considerable valuable information about our social doctrines, Associations, publications, etc. He identifies the founder of the sect as a graduate of a New England college, and the center of the sect as in the town of Lenox, Madison County, "where about 150 persons live together in one house." In regard to the principles of the sect he says that "the Bible is their nominal constitution, and their social doctrine, startling as it is, is taught and the attempt is made to defend it from the scripture. There is no shrinking from the boldest and frankest avowal of their faith and practice."

Three weeks later, a notice in the *Oneida Telegraph* was of another stripe. *The Circular* commended it to general attention as "coming from the best witness on the stand, so far, and establishing one point in our favor: viz., that we are not barbarians in our dealings with outsiders. So far so good":

> The Oneida Community. The article on our fourth page from the N.Y. *Observer*, we present as a matter of news to our readers, who will be interested to see what is said by our neighbors of what is going on in our vicinity. What are the actual practices of the Association to which this article refers, we do not know. *So far as their exterior conduct is concerned, we have always heard the "Community folks" spoken of as an industrious, well-behaved people, and unexceptionable in their dealings with others.* Of their interior arrangements, probably there is less thought and said here in their vicinity than farther away, though all sorts of rumors are afloat —some apparently borne out by the language of their publications— others too revolting to be credited without good testimony.

The *Circular* goes on to correct the *Observer*'s claim that the Oneida Association should be coupled with Mormonism. "This is perhaps the most natural conclusion of a hasty and prejudiced 'observer,'" they write,

> but it is certainly a very mistaken view. At the risk of startling the reverend editor, we must still insist, and shall proceed to prove, that our Society is the farthest opposite of the Mormon polygamic system; that it has, in fact, much less sympathy and congeniality with Mormon ideas than with the ordinary system of which he is the champion.
>
> Mormonism admits a plurality of wives; justified, they say, by the example of the patriarchs of both the old and new Testaments. This is a variation, externally, from the modes of society, but if we look below the form, at the spirit and essence of the institution, we find them very much the same with the world in general. They hold the theory of absolute ownership of persons in marriage; they regard chastity in women (not in men) as an exceedingly frail, perishable thing; and they cultivate in themselves the ferocious bulldog irritability and slave-holder's sense of "honor" in relation to their domestic property that are elsewhere regarded as high virtues.
>
> Now we are fundamentally opposed not only to the form put to the principles of the Mormon establishment: and if anybody is to be classed with those fanatics, it must be the *Observer* rather than us. As a Community we renounce "all enforced property in persons or things," and have no occasion to act as domestic slaveholders. We believe that chastity is as important in men as in women and we do not think it is so frail and contemptible in women as to need a guard of armed jealousy to surround or enforce it. In short, we have no sympathy with the dark, selfish and cruel passions that makes men slave-holders and duelists; that give rise to jealousy, malice and murder and tend to separate every man's interest from that of his brother. The Mormons are evidently under this spirit, as well as the rest of the world in general; but we expect to see it pass away before the dawn of a better time, and that it will be remembered in the future only as we remember the selfish savagery, the stone dunjons and castle keeps of the robber barons of the dark ages.

In spite of this disclaimer, the press in New York City and elsewhere, continued to belabor them. Those in the front line, the Brooklyn family especially, bore the brunt of the attack. As they wrote in the issue of the *Circular* for March 7, 1852: "It is a pretty serious thing to lie under the general and outspoken censure of mankind." It was some consolation to them to remember that it was always the lot of the best to be abused and misunderstood by the world. Conscious of their own innocence, they knew themselves able to withstand whatever defamation the *Observer* chose to indulge in.

On the same page, a two-column article headed "The Past, Present and Future" made a startling announcement. Under the first title, "The Past," they wrote:

> Our position as a Community in regard to marriage and the relation of the sexes has always been more or less an offense to the world and has been much aggravated lately by the gross misrepresentations of sectarian opponents. But it should be observed on the other side, that we have been from the beginning perfectly frank in the avowal of our principles and, as we believe, not illegal in our practices—at least according to the laws of this state. This was evidenced by the fact that for four years we have lived undisturbed. It strikes us as rather ridiculous for the New York *Observer*, at this late day, to call on the Legislature to put down Perfectionism as a new-found heresy.

There was much more to be said, of course, to refute the fierce and various charges of the enemy, and one amusing point claimed that "the special woes of women in connection with children"—that is, unwanted children and uncontrolled pregnancies—"have been nearly extinguished in the Community. The increase of population by birth in our forty families in the last four years, has been considerably less than the progeny of Queen Victoria alone." However, with all that ground of vindication, they were still "looked upon with jealousy and offense by surrounding society." In view of this, they decided to withdraw from their previous position.

> The following manifesto is authorized by the Oneida Association. Editors who love fair-dealing are invited to consider it.
> *It may be understood henceforth that the Oneida Association and all Associations connected with it, have receded from the practical assertion of their views, and formally resumed the marriage morality of the world, submitting themselves to all the ordinances and restrictions of society and law on this subject.*

This concession, they hoped, would give satisfaction and bring peace. They also called attention to the fact that the late disturbances were not caused by any action of the authorities but were merely the work of a newspaper mob.

For the future, they wrote, "We land from our long voyage of exploration, improved and refreshed, with large stores of various experience. The Community organization will remain bound together more firmly than ever by the ties of a common faith and imperishable regard. The Community as a corporate institution is perfectly legal and, in fact, popular where it is best known. We expect now to have our hands loosened for vigorous movements in business and improvement of all kinds, *looking toward the central object of a free press.*"

In the next week's edition, the *Circular*'s editors were able to be amused by the antics of the religious press in response to their late Manifesto:

> The newspapers are getting themselves into a sad tangle of perplexity about the Oneida Community. The extravagant account of its character started by the New York *Observer,* and caught up, echoed and increased by other religious presses, is unsustained by facts, unsustained by the people best acquainted with it, and naturally falls to the ground by its own improbability. It is evident that the Editors are all in the dark, jumping hither and thither at false conclusions, and not likely, as things are going, to come to any satisfactory solution of the problem they are dealing with. We would suggest the propriety, under the circumstances, of all persons interested, particularly the religious editors, stopping where they are and *praying* over the matter. Mere foul-mouthed blustering will amount to nothing, except to complicate the day of settlement with God.

On March 21, under the title, "The March of Events," the editor of the *Circular* found more to say about the recent upheaval. "Evidently the time has come for a more thorough understanding and settlement of the social question, including marriage and family relations. The *Observer* cannot fail to see in the steady stroke of events a providential design to push mankind beyond the old barriers of thought and throw open this primary department of social science to the free play of mind."

As illustration, he calls attention to the series of events relating to the subject: the recent woman's rights movement, Bloomerism, the Mormon excitement ending with the patriarchal system in Utah, "the shock of which, in society, seems to have ended in a laugh." After this there was the scandal of a divorce case, and another case concerned with a German-American, his wife, and his mistress, which "came to a well-known solution—one of the three parties was poisoned, one executed and the third in prison. The whole in consequence of the above-mentioned institution—marriage." After what the Community had suffered, the editor of the *Circular* can scarcely be blamed for adding that without any responsibility of theirs but by the independent direction of Providence, the subject of marriage and its various relations had been the main subject of public thought and discussion during the past winter. "We are not anxious to urge our conclusions upon the world; but we are satisfied that the time is not distant when they will be called for, and the advantage of our education in social matters be appreciated."

On April 4, 1852, the *Circular* noted that the fact of their safe return to the formalities of selfishness seemed to attract as much newspaper attention as the alarming accounts of their previous course had done. Not only the various New York City papers but many provincial ones as well had carried this news and the Association was especially pleased by the courteous attentions of the *Oneida Telegraph*, the *Oneida Chief*, and the Chittenango paper. However, as time went on the whole subject quietly receded from the public eye. Other more secular subjects such as the Whig Convention took its place.

In an article on "The Fear of Man" in the *Circular* of June 27, 1852, the communists merely remarked that although the anathemas of the *Observer* had made faint hearts tremble, they, themselves, had lost nothing but a circle of half-committed friends, and they had found it possible to live in the fiery furnace unharmed.

At the time of the famous manifesto there had been no mention of a *terminus ad quem* for the moratorium of their social practices. The manifesto had simply said "henceforth," which was a definite statement of a beginning, but was there to be an end? In June they said mildly that they were not ashamed of their social principles; "we believe they contemplate a glorious emancipation for man and woman, the highest improvement of the race."

There might be a hint of rebellion in a brief article in the August 4 issue, headed "All Things Continue as They Were." The whole tone is *sotto voce*, almost a whisper, but it says, in fine, that "revolution, progress and the bursting forth of new things have been the rule of the world's history, and the routine which conservatives are so fond of has been the exception." In an article on the *Circular*'s front page three weeks later, August 29, a piece entitled "The Right Kind of Wilfulness," John Humphrey Noyes wrote: "A prodigious change it is, to pass from the laws and precepts of morality to the all-controlling principle of inspiration. A great hue and cry is raised as soon as any one undertakes to make that change. We do promise that we will not oppose the abolition of all customs and fashions unless something better is proposed to take their places. And we further offer for their consideration the fact that we shall not *fall below* the principles or morality recognized in the world; we will either obey them, or rise *above* them; which can only be done by coming into communication with heaven, the source of all true morality."

The close of the first volume of the *Circular* came with the issue of October 31, 1852, and the editor, making no explicit reference either to the ordeal at Utica or the *Observer* affair, admits that the year had been a trying one:

> We have undoubtedly had our full share of personal difficulties and trials to encounter in the years' experience, but the public interest has moved right on and all apparent evil seems now to have passed into general good. On the whole we have lived in a miraculous manner in the past year. With a large family, we have frequently come to the end of our resources, where there was nothing in hand for our next day's dinner, or to buy paper for our next week's printing: but in these circumstances we have been kept from any unpleasant concern, and at the right time, remittances have been received which met all our wants. We can frankly say that we like this method of "living by the day." We never expect to lay up money to rust for future use. We propose now to suspend for a short time during which we shall take a fresh breath of country air, see friends and mature certain improvements for the new volume.

In their next issue two weeks later, they announce the beginning of bi-weekly, instead of weekly, publication, but the only reference to the recent unpleasantness was a squib about the *Observer*. "We notice that the *Observer*, since the close of its quarrel with Henry Ward Beecher, has opened its fire upon Henry

James, a notable writer who proposed loose views on the subject of marriage in the *Tribune*, within a year or two. James replies smartly. We hope they will have a good time. Truth will not die with either of them.''

In January 1853, in an article in the *Circular* entitled "The Bible on Marriage," they gave the rationale for their new position:

> The doctrine that *death* is the legitimate end of the contract of marriage is distinctly conceded by all. Paul and Christ found a way to introduce what may be called a posthumous state by the application of the death of Christ. This doctrine of the believer's death and resurrection by union with Christ was, with the Primitive Church, the very core of the Gospel. They realized that they were past death and were thus delivered from sin and legality. It was the grand apostasy of Christendom that had lost sight of the truth. The Oneida Community would follow Christ and Paul who led them unmistakably to the expectation that marriage would be done away, and the only question was, what next? Complex Marriage was the true answer.

There is no way of knowing whether the communists had come to consider their Manifesto as a mere temporary suspension or a moratorium of the practices which the public had attacked nine months before. However it was, after the publication of their new Platform, the Associations at Oneida and elsewhere returned to the practice of their social theory which they believed in and which they continued to practice almost to the end of their existence.

WISDOM AND RIGHTEOUSNESS

I T IS PROBABLY IMPOSSIBLE for one century—or perhaps even one generation—to understand its predecessor. In other words, what I think my grandfather meant by what he said may be quite different from what he did mean when he said it. For all our piety and wit we can only transcribe the feelings of our ancestors in our own modern alphabet, only decipher what they have written by our own Rosetta Stone. The religious beliefs of John Humphrey Noyes, although they seemed shockingly heterodox to many of his contemporaries a century ago, had at least some modern overtones:

> There are several kinds of belief; a belief of the imagination, of testimony, of the reason and of the senses. Besides these there is another kind which may be called spiritual belief. One spirit can present itself to the perceptions of another and communicate thoughts and persuasions without the intervention of imagination, testimony, reasoning or the senses. While we duly value all the lower evidences of Bible-religion, we are convinced that the belief which is caused by these evidences is but the precursor and auxiliary of spiritual belief. . . . Having ascertained that the Bible is the word of God, the question arises, who shall be our instructor in the word? We answer, inspiration. We find that the Bible itself plainly directs us to inspiration as the ultimate guide of faith.

As a possible answer to us today Noyes had a theory:

The ultimate cause of all evil is an uncreated evil being, as
the ultimate cause of all good is an uncreated good being. If it be
said that evil is nothing but good in disguise, we answer that no evil
is good or can be turned to good in any other than a relative sense.
We find God in all his recorded dealings with men vehemently re-
sisting evil by word and deed. The existence and antagonism of good
and evil are not the results but the antecedents and motives of God's
purpose in creation. The universe was manifestly created for the purpose of furnishing a battle-field whereon the Son of God and the
Devil might come to a decisive conflict.

This was the conflict in which Noyes and his Perfectionist
followers believed themselves to be fighting. Unregenerate man
was wicked because he was enveloped in the spirit of the Devil and
"led captive at his will." Regenerate man was a free moral agent
who had power to act and a knowledge of the right and wrong of
his actions. Spiritual man should discover that there was no natural
repugnance between their spiritual and intellectual natures; they
could work peaceably together in the same yoke and accomplish
much more than either alone. They should "restrain themselves
from disorderly action and exercise common sense, even under the
impulses of the spirit."

Spiritual man should first of all have a loving heart. He
should, however, recognize that Paul distinguished love, or charity,
from that which is commonly accounted charity. "Indeed, it is far
from being that outward bound, bustling quality of character
which usually passes for religious benevolence. It is just that quality which fits a man to live in social contact with his fellow men
without giving offense and without taking offense. It implies a
thorough extinction of selfishness, a perfect appreciation of the
interests of others and the value of peace and a quiet reliance on
the faithfulness of eternal love."

The above is, of course, the briefest possible skeleton of
the body of Noyes's theology, as set forth in *The Berean*. Being
somewhat unregenerate myself, I find parts of *The Berean* rather
hard going, but the little volume published in 1875 by Alfred
Barron for the community, entitled *Home Talks* by John Humphrey Noyes, I find most endearing. It is a collection of "Familiar
Discourses" taken down as spoken and cherished by every Oneida
Community member as the very heart of the community's expressed belief. One of the "Talks" most often mentioned in other

community writing is titled, "Provoking to Love" and it seems to me an epitome of community thinking.

"We are so accustomed to associate wrong with the word 'provoke' that its use in this connection seems a misuse. But we have only to use the proper stimulus, and love can be provoked as certainly as wrath. Devise occasion and we shall see it *flash out* and retort like a burst of anger. The art of provoking to wrath seems to come by nature; men practice it without 'forethought' but some consideration is required to make us successful in provoking love. We are to consider not ourselves, but one another. We miss happiness when we pursue it too directly. When we would pour it into *another's* cup, it overflows into our own."

In the matter of health, John Noyes seems to have preceded Mary Baker Eddy, since his first faith cure occurred in Putney in the case of Harriet Hall in 1847, an affair which roused the fury of his fellow townsmen against him and which, it must be confessed, seems to have been a sort of now-you-see-it-now-you-don't business, since the patient recovered and relapsed not once but several times. This, however, did not discourage Noyes or his followers. For more than twenty years the Oneida Communists lived staunchly undoctored and unmedicined.

As Noyes assured them in another of his *Home Talks* they should not rely on exercise, diet, ventilation, and all that, to give them that positive health which repulses disease, but betake themselves to the divine mysteries of exorcism and baptism into Christ. True ruggedness, he declared, like true righteousness, did not come by self-works but was a gift from God. "Diet, ventilation and exercise are only assistants of divine health. They have never saved anybody from old age and never will."

"In seeking the ruggedness of God we must understand the order in which he works. Our nature is like a nest of four boxes. The inner box is the spiritual part, the next is the intellectual, the next is the moral and the outer box is physical. God will begin to renew us by giving us ruggedness in the spirit, which will enable us to face all devils without fear and live in contact with them without contamination. Then he will give us ruggedness of understanding which fears no argument and overcomes all delusions. Then he will give us ruggedness of moral nature which is strong enough to keep its resolutions and submit to no condemnation. And, finally, through all these mediates, he will give us ruggedness of physical health."

His attitude toward old age is equally bracing:

Old age should not be considered a thing to be reverenced without question, more than any other disease. Old age is, in my imagination, something entirely separate from anybody I call my friend or the friend of Christ, and I desire more and more to see it separated from the alliances which make it respectable. It must be indicted and brought to trial; let it have a fair trial before God and man and receive its final verdict. If it is a thing which we are bound to reverence and bow down to, let us bow down; but if not, let us raise an insurrection and turn it out. Old people ought not to grumble at this conclusion. The very best thing that can be done for them is to start a crusade against the spirit of old age. If they can do nothing for themselves, they ought to be hopeful and cheer on the work of others because they are to be emancipated by it.

It is common for people at a certain age to make up their minds that they have seen their best days. This idea becomes to them a continual undertone, or what our writers call the "minor mode in music," the "everlasting wail." I know that I have not seen my best days. I expect to do a great deal more work during the twenty years to come than I have done during the twenty years past, so on forever.

On another occasion, in the *Circular*, August 14, 1865, he gave specific directions for accomplishing this end:

In order to keep your spirits bright, in order to maintain a state of ripe vivacity, you must be just as busy with the great purposes of heroic accomplishment as you were at 22, or as true, heroic youthfulness always is. You may judge your spirit by this test: If you are saying to yourself, "Well, I cannot accomplish anything for I shall not live but a little while; I am getting to be old; my best days are gone; great purposes are for the young and I have got by them." If that is the way you are talking, you are surrendering to old age and the devil. The way you should talk is, "I am 22 years old now and never will be any older; as great a field of hopefulness and improvement opens to me now as there did at 22, and my heart is as open to great plans now as it ever was. The idea that I have seen my best days come to their end is all humbug. The heart that is open to God's plans and inspiration will have immortality, and its purposes will have no end."

John Humphrey Noyes, founder of the Oneida Community, photo probably around 1870.

Apparently this advice was taken by one member, who said he thought the best way to overcome old age (which was nothing but a bad habit) was to ignore it.

The community's religion, for all its piety, had a strong, invigorating quality which often came out in their criticisms. For example, Mr. I. was criticized for regarding Christ only as the Lamb of God, perfectly yielding and docile to his father but quite overlooking his character as the Lion of Judah. Mr. I. was advised to rouse some of the Lion in himself. He had once knocked a man down and it was hoped that he would now come up to scratch and do the same thing to this principality that had hindered the work of truth and righteousness.

In one of his *Home Talks* entitled "Help Yourself," Noyes wrote:

> You have not, as a single person, to face millions of other persons, but your one spirit is to meet that one spirit in single combat; and all that is wanted is more courage, faith and power in you than there is in that spirit. "One shall chase a thousand and two put ten thousand to flight." No matter how great the number, your single spirit is sufficient to cope with the whole. . . . David, with the inspiration of a better and stronger principality, slew Goliath with a stone. . . . We can conquer the world in the same way. . . . Know the words which Isaiah puts in the mouth of his righteous hero: "I looked and there was none to help; and I wondered that there was none to uphold; therefore *mine own arm brought salvation unto me and my fury upheld me.*" So we shall find that the wonder of despair is the very crisis in which God's omnipotence breaks forth.

Certainly "the wonder of despair" had been often the experience of the young John Noyes and during the years of his prime it seemed still to uphold him. Nevertheless it took courage to meet the world, as he said, in single combat. But what of that? As he told his son, Theodore, in the *Circular* of July 28, 1867, the true kind of improvement was to be doing something all the time that required courage.

The Oneida Communists tried, for thirty years, to keep this in mind. Improvement. They had improved their dwellings. They had improved their living conditions. They had improved their financial condition. These, to the faithful, were minor matters. Had they improved in selflessness? Had they improved in

Harriet Holton Noyes ("Mother Noyes") married John Humphrey Noyes in Putney, Vermont, in 1838, and was his devoted lifelong companion.

loving kindness? Had they improved in devotion to God? These were the important matters. And next in importance, had they borne and brought up their children in the love and admonition of the Lord? For this they prayed.

At one time, after "discussion and investigation of the parental relation," they drew up a list of General Principles. The first of these principles may shock the modern child-centered parent. "The love and care of children in parents should not supplant or interfere with their love as man and woman. Amativeness takes precedence of philoprogenitiveness, and parental feeling becomes a usurpation when it crowds out a passion which is relatively its superior."

Another principle sounds a faintly Calvinistic note. "Parents should not sacrifice the spiritual welfare of their children to their mere bodily comfort." But the communists' New England forebears might not have approved of another: "Rearing children should be carried on in connection with self-culture, and the appetite for improvement, and should not be allowed to seriously encroach upon them."

One principle was kept well in mind—communizing the children; making them the property of the whole Community as completely as they did with all their other possessions. In the World, each mother naturally had the care of all her children's clothes. In the community, all the children's clothes were the responsibility of those in charge of the Juvenile Department, "the mothers," as the *Circular* reported, "gladly consenting." The children themselves took part in this communization. "Each one brought his store of toys and made a large collection to be used by all in common. They were very enthusiastic about it and enjoyed the draft they got of the Pentecostal Spirit as much as anybody. No one now says 'me' and 'mine' but 'ours' and 'we.'"

Perfectionists. Remember that these people sought perfection: "purity of heart and the answer of a good conscience toward God," John Humphrey Noyes replied to his attackers as a young convert in 1834. Toward the end of his life, when he was questioned about his great experiment in human eugenics, Stirpiculture, he had a new answer to the problem in the *Circular* of December 6, 1875:

"The question is, how is there ever going to be an end of suffering or troubles of the flesh as a means of teaching us wisdom? We see that we have to learn lesson after lesson by terrible experience; generation after generation passes away with people arriving at real wisdom only at the end of their lives when they are just quitting the world; that one generation does not love another, but the second comes up just as foolish as the first and has to go through the same troubles; worrying along through life and finally getting to be wise just when they are ready to drop into the grave.

East front of Mansion House, early 1870s.

The question arises, how long must that last? How long must we be born and grow up fools and only grow wise by suffering, as our fathers did before us? I can tell you just when all this repeating of troubles over and over is going to end. It will be when wisdom and righteousness are fixed in the blood, so that lessons which the parents have learned by experience, the children will have in them when they are born. If you can tell me when that will be, you can tell when the end of all these tribulations is coming, for it won't come until then. Lord, hasten the day, is my prayer."

It did not come in his time and has not, thus far, in ours. Perhaps some new community will yet be able to supply the answer. Certainly all of us join in his prayer, "Lord, hasten the day."

ONEIDA COMMUNITY PROFILES

was composed in 10-point IBM Selectric Century Medium and leaded two points
by Metricomp Studios, Inc.;
with display type in VIP Century Expanded by Dix Typesetting Co., Inc.;
printed on Hammermill 55-pound Lock Haven by Vicks Lithograph and Printing Corp.;
Smyth-sewn and bound over boards in Holliston Crown Linen by
Vail-Ballou Press, Inc.;
and published by

SYRACUSE UNIVERSITY PRESS
Syracuse, New York 13210